Finding Your Power, Passion, and Purpose Through Self-Awareness and Self-Love

CHANTELLE RENEE

Copyright © 2017 Chantelle Renee.

Cover design by Chantelle Renee, Silviya Yordanova,
Jonathan Brice Lyman, and Gary V. Tenuta.

Interior Graphics/Art Credits:
- Office of Masaru Emoto, LLC -
- Andrew Kukla, Silviya Yordanova, and Jonathan Brice Lyman -

All rights reserved. No part of this book may be used or reproduced by any means, graphic, electronic, or mechanical, including photocopying, recording, taping or by any information storage retrieval system without the written permission of the author except in the case of brief quotations embodied in critical articles and reviews.

Scripture taken from the Holy Bible, NEW INTERNATIONAL VERSION®. Copyright © 1973, 1978, 1984, 2011 by Biblica, Inc. All rights reserved worldwide. Used by permission. NEW INTERNATIONAL VERSION® and NIV® are registered trademarks of Biblica, Inc. Use of either trademark for the offering of goods or services requires the prior written consent of Biblica US, Inc.

Balboa Press books may be ordered through booksellers or by contacting:

Balboa Press
A Division of Hay House
1663 Liberty Drive
Bloomington, IN 47403
www.balboapress.com
1 (877) 407-4847

Because of the dynamic nature of the Internet, any web addresses or links contained in this book may have changed since publication and may no longer be valid.

The views expressed in this work are solely those of the author and do not necessarily reflect the views of the publisher, and the publisher hereby disclaims any responsibility for them.

The author of this book does not dispense medical advice or prescribe the use of any technique as a form of treatment for physical, emotional, or medical problems without the advice of a physician, either directly or indirectly. The intent of the author is only to offer information of a general nature to help you in your quest for emotional and spiritual well-being. In the event you use any of the information in this book for yourself, which is your constitutional right, the author and the publisher assume no responsibility for your actions.

Print information available on the last page.

ISBN: 978-1-5043-9072-9 (sc)
ISBN: 978-1-5043-9074-3 (hc)
ISBN: 978-1-5043-9073-6 (e)

Library of Congress Control Number: 2017917619

Balboa Press rev. date: 12/11/2017

Dedication

I dedicate this book to the unseen, the unheard, the unloved, the grieving, and the hurting. The lost, the seekers and the non-believers, even the deceivers. For anyone who is struggling in their life, don't give up. You are loved beyond measure. You may not believe this, but please try: open to receive the love that is yours. You are a child of light, destined to shine brightly.

"You're far more powerful than you may have been led to believe. It is time to remember your greatness as a powerful, eternal being—a creator, a direct reflection of All That Is And Ever Has Been. It is time to stand confidently in your power."
—Chantelle Renee

Contents

Dedication v
List of Illustrations xiii
Note to Reader xv
Preface xvii
Acknowledgments xxi
Introduction xxiii
   We Are Here to Create History, Not Repeat It xxiii

Chapter 1   The Energetic, Living Universe 1
Chapter 2   The Universal Natural Laws 5
   A Brief History of New Thought and Hermetic Thought 5
   Thoughts are Things 9
   Think Big – Using the Twelve Principles 13
   Trust the Universe 15
      The Law of Divine Oneness (Immutable) 16
      The Law of Vibration (Immutable) 17
      The Law of Action (Immutable) 18
      The Law of Correspondence (Immutable) 19
      The Law of Cause and Effect 20
      The Law of Compensation 20
      The Law of Attraction 21
      The Law of Perpetual Transmutation of Energy 21
      The Law of Relativity 22
      The Law of Polarity 23

    The Law of Rhythm 24
    The Law of Gender..24
    Taking Action – Putting the Laws and the Science to
    Work for You 27

Chapter 3   Earth – The Cosmic College 33
    Karma – Stepping out of the Karmic Cycle...........................37
    Releasing Karmic Bonds 40

Chapter 4   Energy Awareness 43
    Universal Energy...44
    The Torus 45
    Cymatics – The Science of Frequency 47
    Energy Anatomy – The Subtle Body 51
    The Aura 52
    The Seven Major Chakras – Part I – Alignment to
    Source Energy...54
    The Seven Major Chakras – Part II – Healing
    with the Chakras 57
        The 1st Chakra – the Root Chakra (Muladhara)............59
        The 2nd Chakra – the Sacral Chakra (Svadhisthana)......60
        The 3rd Chakra – the Solar Plexus Chakra (Manipura)......62
        The 4th Chakra – the Heart Chakra (Anahata) 63
        The 5th Chakra – the Throat Chakra (Vishuddha) 65
        The 6th Chakra – the Third Eye Chakra (Anja) 67
        The 7th Chakra – the Crown Chakra (Sahasrāra)...........68
    Spirit Manifested in the Material World 70
    Are You Ready to Flow? 76
    Ten Easy Ways to Empower Yourself: 77

Chapter 5   Intuition – Our Soul's Navigation 79
    Exercise..80
    Feel into your Heart Space 84

Your Clair Senses 84
    Clairvoyance..85
    Clairaudience...85
    Clairsentience 86
    Clairscent 86
    Clairtangency 86
    Clairgustance...86
    Clairempathy...86
    Claircognizance 87
    Channel/Channeling 87
Working with Your Guides 89

Chapter 6   Breaking the Chains – Limiting Core Beliefs..........93
Be Present with Yourself...96
Exercise..96
Core Beliefs...97
Shifting Your Core Beliefs Worksheet 99
Journaling... 102
The Ultimate Questions to Ask When
    Challenging a Belief: 103

Chapter 7   Relationships: Mirrors for our Expansion.............. 105
Practicing Non-Judgement.. 108

Chapter 8   Taming the Ego 113
Ten Ways to Tame Your Ego:..115
Self-Love and Spiritual Prosperity 117
Take the Other Road 121
Open Your Heart... 122
Practice Gratitude 127
Embrace Life – Love Yourself!.. 128
Four Practical Exercises to Learn to Love Yourself 128
Create Your Future... 131

Chapter 9   Creating with Emotion 133
    Epigenetics and Your Emotional World 134
    The Tyranny of Emotion 137
    The Power of Feeling 140
    The Emotional Scale 142
    Solitude.. 145

Chapter 10   Law of Attraction... 147
    Reprogramming... 151

Chapter 11   Your Action Plan – Manifesting your Dreams 155

Chapter 12   Conclusion... 163

Works Cited – Reading List 167
Notes 173
About the Author 183

List of Illustrations

- Awakening - Page 36
- Energy Human Absorption Model - Page 44
- Love and Fear Torus - Page 45
- Love and Love Torus - Page 47
- Dr. Emoto – Water Image - Page 49
- Human Aura Energy Layers - Page 52
- Child with Chakras - Page 55
- Muladhara Chakra Symbol - Page 59
- Svadhisthana Chakra Symbol - Page 60
- Manipura Chakra Symbol - Page 62
- Anahata Chakra Symbol - Page 63
- Vishuddha Chakra Symbol - Page 65
- Anja Chakra Symbol - Page 67
- Sahasrāra Chakra Symbol - Page 68
- Intuition, Internal Guidance - Page 79
- Chained - Page 94
- Relationship Mirrors - Page 105
- The Flux and Flow of Human Emotions and Feelings - Page 139

Note to Reader

In this book, in order to be all-inclusive regarding religious and spiritual belief systems, I have referred to *"God"* as *God*. It is my hope that this symbolic usage will welcome and include all believers and seekers—those who believe in the Christian God in heaven as Lord of all creation, those who believe in the God of other monotheistic religions, and those who believe in God the creator as Universal Spirit. If you believe in God as chaos, God as intrinsic in the human spirit, or even in God-as-goddess, this *God* is also yours. In this spirit of inclusiveness, I refer to *God* throughout this book as "He/he," "She/she," and as "it." Please read *God* as the God of your own heart, soul, and faith system. Thank you.
—Chantelle

Preface

Welcome, All Souls of All Faiths.

There comes a point in everyone's life when we ask these questions:

- Who am I?
- Where did I come from?
- Why am I here?
- Who—or what—is *God*?

I came into the world knowing a few things. I knew that *God* was not judgmental, I knew that those who held racist attitudes and separatist beliefs were ignorant, and I knew that the universe was on my side. I can't explain how I knew. I just did.

I have never been able to abide what others have shared with me regarding the meaning of life and being human, especially what I was told by those who purported to speak on behalf of *God*. I have always rebelled against "man-made" rules. I have felt safe and secure with my own connection to *God* and was never willing to hand it over to anyone.

Having a close communion with spirit has served my life in many ways. I am truly thankful for the gift of life and try to not take it for granted.

My curiosity about creation has been an ongoing love affair, a daily communion in which I seek a deeper understanding of the questions above. When I get still, when I concentrate deeply and move into my heart, I can get lost within the abyss of the collective mind—the mind that is everything, everywhere, and everyone. It feels like a hurricane of emotion, creation, and destruction, there in the heartbeat of the infinite.

I know that when I am in that place, I am observing not only the infinite chasm of the cosmos, but I am also observing myself. I know too, that the observation of self is the observation of *God*—*God* that is you, *God* that is me.

My inner quest has always been to understand life's greatest mysteries. All my life, I have questioned, I have pondered, and I have sought union with the oneness of creation. So, when I first had a *Eureka!* moment and realized that I am—we all are—one with the universe, I felt sad. In that stillness, when I finally discovered the secret of creation, my reality and self-identity slowly unraveled. Yet at the same time, this truth gifted me, shifted me, and destroyed my perceived vision of myself. It handed me the power to align with the Divine and to take full responsibility for my life, my experience, and my creations.

And so, the story goes—not just for me, but for all of us. We are all one, with one another and one with creation. *We are *God*.* We will eternally remember and forget this, remember and forget, over and over again, and we will spend our lives continually discovering and rediscovering the majesty of our own Divinity.

This means you.

You see, to be awake is but a dream. We are dreaming a dream in which we are forever seeking, eternally reaching for higher states of being. I have found the bliss of oneness in the stillness of my heart. I am awake. Now, I am dreaming consciously—dreaming about eternity. I am grateful for the gifts that creation has bestowed upon me and upon you. Eternity is a cosmic sea of infinite possibilities. I will dive deeply, fearlessly into the unknown shores of self-discovery, forever.

Will you join me?

When I was young, I longed for a book that would guide me through my exploration of potential truths and spiritual-empowerment. Since I never found that book, I wrote *this book*—and now, I am handing it to you. My hope is that this book will help you to create a space for your own Divine exploration, that it will inspire you to seek higher states of being, that it will help you to heal patterns of pain, and empower you to think beyond the borrowed beliefs and preconceived ideologies that many of us have blindly adopted as our own. My hope is that when you read this book, and embrace the wisdom in its pages, you will reclaim your sacred energy and manifest the life of your choosing. My dream is that this book will help you to cultivate peace within yourself and to awaken those around you.

Within these pages are my personal perspectives as well as ancient wisdom that has been kept secret for millennia. As you absorb these teachings and dive into your subconscious mind to challenge any self-limiting beliefs you may hold, I invite you to write your thoughts and revelations down. In the back of the book are blank pages for you to use. Journaling frequently as you move through this book will help you to illuminate any self-sabotaging patterns that are holding you back from becoming the best version of yourself. As you ponder the wisdom in this book, hold the intention that you wish to transcend your current state of being and move into a state of wholeness.

I sincerely hope you find this book to be a springboard into remembering and reclaiming who you really are—a child of light, a gift from the Most High. Many seekers have achieved enlightenment on their own. It is my hope that together, we can all obtain enlightenment and in so doing, raise the collective vibration of this planet to the benefit of all of creation.

Merging into Wholeness

"With each shift in consciousness, your inner world changes as your view of the outer world changes. The process of spiritual expansion is serious—it comes with a cost. You will never again be the person you once thought you were. The distractions you once participated in will begin to fade. As you create a quiet space in which you begin to hear existence, solitude calls you. You may feel lonely—do not be afraid—you are merging into your wholeness from the illusion of separateness."
—Chantelle Renee

Acknowledgments

This book has been made possible by so many people dear to my heart, I can hardly find the words to express my deep and unwavering gratitude.

To my children, Jay and Savannah, you inspire me, challenge me, and bless me with your beings. I have grown exponentially through the gift of mothering you. Thank you. I love and cherish you.

To Jason, my lifelong love, you are a man among men, truly an incredible human being. You have stood by me through all things, supported me in every way possible, and loved me. You accept my unconventional philosophy and still choose to grow with me. May we continue to love one another and flourish together—and most of all, may we continue to enjoy each other each and every day.

To my family—my father, mother, and brother—I love you and appreciate you dearly. To my mother and father in-law, you have been a blessing in my life since I was seventeen. Thank you, from the bottom of my heart, for all you have done for our family. I love and appreciate you.

To my readers—and especially to those of you who have been with me since I began to share my spiritual ideas online—*thank you all*. Your belief in the messages I have shared has fueled my focus to complete this book. The outpouring of love and gratitude I receive from you shines a light on my path. Thanks to you, I have found my life's purpose—to assist others in remembering our Divine connection to all things.

To my editor, Michael K. Ireland, you have been a gift to this project. Your talent and deep spiritual understanding have brought *Aligning with the Divine* to a level that I could not have achieved alone. I appreciate everything you taught me—and how you pushed me to grow as a writer.

To Gary, Andrew, Silviya, and Jonathan—the graphic artists who worked with me on this project—thank you for sharing your talent and your expertise, and for seeing my vision so clearly. I honor and treasure you.

Last—but certainly not least—thanks to *God*, the Holy Spirit, Jesus, and the Angels. You have been my inspiration since childhood. Your constant presence gave me a confidence that has fueled my unwavering faith in humanity.

Bless you all.
Chantelle

Introduction

"Seeking truth is the key to discovering life's greatest mysteries. However, we must not cling too tightly to any truth, as there will always be more truth awaiting discovery."
—Chantelle Renee

We Are Here to Create History, Not Repeat It

We live in amazing times. Many people are awakening from their spiritual slumber and are seeking the deeper meanings of existence. Many are discovering that we are far more powerful than we have been led to believe—we are a direct reflection of creation; eternal beings of energy and light.

It is a time of great growth in human consciousness, a time to reclaim our power and to align with the Divine. I hope the ideas in this book will inspire you to join me on a path towards spiritual awareness and empowerment. I hope you travel well on this quest of awakening to your true power—the power that lies dormant within you.

This book reveals some of the universe's best-kept, ancient secrets. It will serve you as you learn to cultivate compassion, to understand your fellow human beings more deeply, and to nurture your own inner peace and spiritual prosperity. As you read this book, you will learn, through simple, practical steps:

- how to use the laws of physics to manifest a life of your choosing,
- how to understand the human body's energy systems,
- how to practice energy awareness,
- how to navigate your emotional state,
- how to love yourself on a deeper level,
- how to free yourself from self-sabotaging patterns that prevent your life from flowing in harmony with creation,
- how to become self-aware, and
- how to create with emotion.

By reading this book you will:

- become more in tune with your intuition—your own direct connection with spirit,
- delve into your subconscious mind,
- challenge your borrowed beliefs,
- free yourself from the bondage of a limiting perspective,
- review scientific evidence of the power of intention and thought,
- discover that all of your relationships serve your spiritual progression,
- learn to tame your ego and practice non-judgement, and
- receive a "Manifesting" action plan.

This book is a resource you can turn to again and again to assist you in your sacred journey of exploration and spiritual expansion. My hope is that this book will serve you in your awakening, that it will empower you to connect directly to the Divine, and lead you to your life's passion and purpose.

Fueled by the clarity of your intentions, may you pursue your dreams fearlessly and manifest abundantly! It is a thrilling time to be alive!

The cosmos creates cycles, offering us endless opportunities to stop and reflect, and to move more deeply into our spiritual selves. But are we ready to break out of our old ways of seeing the world in order to seek truth—or do we want to stay locked in a reality in which we have accepted others' limited notions as our own? Do we carry in our hearts a modern perception of reality—or are we grounded in the belief systems of our ancestors?

Are you ready to let go of your old ways and embrace a new reality? If this feels challenging for you, I invite you to soften your energy and remain open. Your soul chose this lifetime, after all, it's just a matter of remembering that, and stepping out of the illusion you have been in. This can be a great challenge for many people as we can easily become lazy, content to live in the comfort of our borrowed beliefs. Breaking out of these outdated beliefs can be uncomfortable—but remember—through discomfort, we can discover a deeper truth of what it means to be alive, here and now, in the twenty-first millennium.

We are all seekers, here to create history, not to repeat it! We must take responsibility for our own spiritual transformation. We must let go of what we think we know and be present, in the here and now. No matter who we are, we all have something to contribute to humanity, something that can benefit our own forward movement, something that can raise us up into a higher understanding of what it means to be alive. By becoming mentally and spiritually strong, by consciously living life, we can elevate the vibration of the planet. Don't you want to be a part of something bigger than you, something that is going to take this whole planet to the next level? If you do, let go of the past, embrace the now—that is the way to our golden future! Our past is meant to guide us, not enslave us.

The time has come for us to empower each other, to go above and beyond the limitations that we have been conditioned by our forbearers to accept. Many of us will be called to rise, but only those who are brave enough to change will rise.

We must choose consciously to transform ourselves. We must build bridges instead of walls, we must dissolve the illusion that we are separate from one another—and instead we must anchor ourselves in a new vibration. We must begin to live collectively, as a tribe, as a community. We each hold the keys to one another's unfolding—mentally, emotionally, physically, and spiritually. As we open our hearts and minds to one another, we discover that our true power lies within one another. We are a family—a global clan of light workers.

The way we will change the future is through loving one another and through cultivating compassion for one another. Historically, generation after generation, we have seen patterns of self-destruction. Hurt people hurt others. Disempowered people disempower others. This ends now—it ends with us. Now, to create history, we will meet each other in the depths of transparency, humility, and vulnerability. We will meet each other with forgiveness, love, and compassion.

As we begin to focus, together, on solutions instead of on the problems of the world, we will begin to transcend the old ways—the ways of duality, separateness, and division. The most powerful solution to the world's ills is to evolve our consciousness—not only individually, but collectively. The more human beings on this planet who align to our sovereign, eternal nature, the more of us who embrace the reality that we came here to love—to experience, to expand, and to explore—the more our societies will transform, from the inside out. As each individual finds peace within themselves, they will in turn assist the collective to find its peace as well. Each newly-empowered human being will lead us closer to an empowered humanity.

To rise together, we must understand and accept that all perspectives are valid in the eyes of creation. All of us serve as part of an evolutionary expansion of consciousness and of creation itself. We must step out of our egos and into our hearts, we must foster conversations that co-create real change through compassion. Remaining open, truly listening to others is how we will create and rebuild our society. We must meet each other unconditionally, honoring our sameness, instead of fueling our perceived differences. This is the evolutionary path of any species which seeks to thrive collectively. So, never stop planting seeds of love and truth, never stop seeking healing!

A big misconception has kept us focused on the material world and not focused on the world we cannot perceive with our human senses. That misconception is that *our physical reality is the highest reality*. It is not—in fact, we abide in an endless sea of cosmic energy that manifests abundantly, in all directions, within multiple realities. If we keep our hearts and minds open to the infinite possibilities available to us in our universe, without limiting our greatest potentiality, we can reclaim our sacred majesty.

To do this, we must learn to give and receive freely. We must step out of 'lack mentality' and embrace the concept that this universe is abundant. Giving and receiving love freely creates the balance and harmony for all of creation to thrive equally. Coming together in solidarity will create a brand new, collective reality with unbounded possibilities.

So, as a society, as a family, we must work together, so that we may rise together. Our species' very survival depends upon our ability to adapt, to change, and to empower ourselves. Together, we can co-create a world united in love, peace, and harmony.

"But how can we do this?" you might ask. "How? The world is in such dire circumstances. How can we turn it around?"

Starting now, question everything that you have been taught can't be done. Banish the idea that anything is impossible. Everything is possible! It's time for each of us to reclaim our birthright—we are infinitely creative, the world is filled with unbounded possibilities, and we must become dedicated to releasing the limitations that we have been conditioned to accept. We must embrace the fact that we are one with the whole universe—we are immeasurable, vast, and powerful! We are one with our planet and our planet is one with us.

Much of the chaos within the world stems directly from our disconnection to our higher self, source, and nature. Our life force has become fragmented. We must heal ourselves, we must heal each other. We must become conscious parents, raising conscious children. We must break the generational patterns that have kept the human family from becoming fully who we are really meant to be.

We have been gifted with a vision, the wonder of life, and the miracle of being one with all of creation. As we begin to accept our inherent power, we step away from our shadows and into the light of creation. We must, each of us, walk through this life fearlessly, lovingly, with gratitude, remaining always in the present moment, with peace in our hearts.

By doing our own personal energetic and spiritual work, we are supporting humanity's transformation, from the inside out. The foundation of our future—true, lasting change—depends upon you and me. Your evolution is our revolution.

> "By taking responsibility for your own spiritual awakening, you impact humanity's awakening."
> —Chantelle Renee

1

The Energetic, Living Universe

> "All matter originates and exists only by virtue of a force.... We must assume behind this force the existence of a conscious and intelligent Mind. This Mind is the matrix of all matter."
> —Max Planck

Do you realize that you are a creative entity, infinitely powerful, and responsible for manifesting into reality everything that you see in your own world? You are!

In this chapter, we will delve into the phenomenon of the energetic universe. Have you ever considered how your individual energy field ties in with the energy of the vast universe? Listed below are some ideas to help you reflect upon this notion. Use the Notes pages included at the end of this book, or take some quiet time with your journal and meditate on each of the following concepts. Write down your insights and intuitive perceptions. As you sit with each idea listed below, remember the adage, *As Above, So Below*.

- The scientific insights of the first verse of The Bible are profound. In Genesis 1:1, it says that God created the heavens and the earth. From this, we can ascertain that *time*, *space*, and *matter* were created by a Supreme Being:

    - In the beginning (Time),
    - *God* created the heavens (Space),
    - and the earth (Matter).

    The physical world that *God* created 'in the beginning' has an incredibly efficient and effective design. *God's* creation is wondrous, miraculous, harmonious, magical—and above all, mysterious. Despite everything our scientists know about the true origins and mechanics of our physical universe, we have only begun to scratch the surface of understanding the secret, creative mechanics of our universe.

    Inspired by this Divine mystery, we each set out on our soul's journey of exploration, expansion, and evolution. We are, after all, Divine beings, having a physical experience. Can you see that you, a spirit experiencing time and space, are fully capable of creating matter? *God* the Creator lives both within us and outside of us, and extends his unconditional love and creativity to us. Can you acknowledge that *you are *God*.*? Can you accept that you can manifest anything that you wish to have...simply by thinking and feeling it into being?

- We are eternal, intelligent energy. Our awareness that everything is energy offers us the opportunity to enter our power as creators of our own experience. Everything is connected and all is one—this is the Divine Law of Oneness.

In Matthew 5: 14-16 it says:
You are the light of the world. A town built on a hill cannot be hidden. Neither do people light a lamp and put it under a bowl. Instead they put it on its stand, and it gives light to everyone in the house. In the same way, let your light shine before others, that they may see your good deeds and glorify your Father in heaven.

What this means is that as the light of the world, you are made up, in your DNA, of *Divine light*, of electromagnetic fields of *energy*. Open your heart and mind to this cosmic connection; the cosmos run through your veins and every fiber of your being. Let your Divine light shine out for all to see!

- As we look through the lens of our human eyes, we think we can see the whole world. But quantum physics has confirmed that space and time are illusions of perception and that what we perceive with our five-senses human system is not the only reality. When we look at the quantum electromagnetic spectrum, for example, we realize that we are only seeing a tiny percentage of what is really going on around us. We are constantly giving out and receiving frequencies that we cannot perceive with our human senses. This is why it is important to strengthen your own intuition and practice energy awareness. Divine energy surrounds us at all times and we have the power—through our awareness and intention—of pulling unlimited amounts of pure source energy from the unified field.

When we explore the concept that science and spirituality are connected forces, we open up many new avenues of thought and become empowered to align with the Divine as extensions of *God*, as creative entities—as the crux of creation itself. As we begin to merge spirituality and science, we come to a whole new understanding of our power as energetic, vibrational beings. We realize that the universe is always working on our behalf. By engaging fully with and embracing Divine energy, we can step into our power as creators.

All matter is energy condensed to a slow vibration; we are all one consciousness experiencing itself. The universe works in perfect harmony, and to flow with it (and not against it), we must clean up the disharmony within ourselves. So, do not resist your power—tap in, allow, and flow with the energy of the cosmos!

2

The Universal Natural Laws

"Now think about the Universal Law. It reflects to you exactly and precisely what you put out. If your thought-forms say, "I haven't got a clue about what I want," the Universal Law is going to say, "Listen, mate, if you haven't got a clue, neither have I."
—Stuart Wilde

A Brief History of New Thought and Hermetic Thought

Those of us who embrace the New Thought realities of our twenty-first century are entering a new vibration, we are transcending our past limitations and opening up to the limitless possibilities of creation. As we have seen, there is an endless sea of cosmic energy available to us—and it allows us to manifest abundantly. So, keep your heart and mind open to receiving your infinite, limitless, creative potential!

As an adherent of New Thought concepts, you have no doubt discovered that there are numerous powerful, life-changing, ancient insights that were not taught to you in school. These archaic ideas, known generally as "Hermetic principles," are the basis of the New Thought (or, as some call it, the "New Age") movement. These spiritual principles, universal laws, and laws of nature govern every aspect of our world, the universe, and the entire cosmos. They are as real as the law of physics (in fact they are *the metaphysical laws of physics!*) and they play an intricate part in your life—whether you are aware of it or not.

In a nutshell, the Hermetic principles are grounded in the mystical and secret teachings of ancient India, Egypt, and Greece, societies which employed sacred geometry, ancient cosmology, and natural philosophy to confirm their belief that the universe (and all of creation) has its source in an intelligent, Divine design, and that this design was, is, and ever shall be, the source of all.

Thus, the same age-old, universal laws that guided and determined the lives and fates of our ancestors are the self-same laws that we can use for self-actualization, to follow our dreams and to fulfill our lives, passion, and purpose.

In this chapter, we look at a little bit of arcane history—and a little bit of modern history, to discover that when we embrace the principles and belief systems that were used by our forbearers over 5,000 years ago, and apply them to our modern lives, we can become creators with the Divine! But we do not need to become historians of Egyptian philosophy or ancient Greek religions to tap into this wisdom, for our modern philosophers and thinkers have already done all the work for us. Take the powerful "New Age" concepts of the *Law of Attraction* and the idea that *Thoughts are Things*, for example. The late Dr. Wayne Dyer talked about these theories in his *Power of Intention* books; Esther Hicks, Jerry Hicks, and Abraham expounded upon them in their *Law of Attraction* series; and Rhonda Byrne addressed them in her famous book and movie, *The Secret*. Countless other human potential writers have played upon these concepts too: Neville Goddard, Bob Proctor, Pam Grout, Eric Pearl—all have embraced these inspirational ideas.

Their books explain that if you put these notions into practice you can improve your life and manifest your destiny. Their books are filled with unique, imaginative ideas about routines and systems you can use to make your dreams a reality—and they are all based on the conviction that the Law of Attraction is a fundamental law that works in tandem with the concept that *thoughts are things*. When you look a little deeper, you realize that many of these authors are actually writing about the seven principles of Hermetic Thought!

The principle that *thoughts are things* was first modernized by the insightful, best-selling author Napoleon Hill in his landmark book *Think and Grow Rich*. First published in 1937, it sold twenty million copies and taught ordinary people how to make a fortune by thinking positively and strategically. *Think and Grow Rich* was based upon Hill's earlier book, the 1928 *Law of Success* which he wrote at the behest of the great Dale Carnegie, author of the blockbuster book *How to Win Friends and Influence People* and the first twentieth century thinker to introduce the idea that *thoughts are things*. Carnegie's book sold five million copies in twenty years.

It is a testament to their enduring wisdom that these books have captured the attention of generations of truth seekers. While the language and tone of Hill's and Carnegie's books speak to the sentiments and worldviews of a different era, Dyer, Byrne, the Hicks's, and others have taken these basic ideas and reworked them for the twenty-first century, adding in self-improvement tips and tricks to expand on the basic principles expressed by Hill and Carnegie.

But these transformational ideas were not original to these authors—and that is important in the context of our quantum exploration. Carnegie likely got his ideas from nineteenth century essayist, philosopher, and poet Ralph Waldo Emerson, who is thought of as a "grandfather of the New Age." As a leader of the Transcendentalist Movement, it was he who propounded the idea of "the power of positive thinking." But the idea was not original to Emerson, either, for it was founded in the wisdom of the Neoplatonists of the early centuries CE and the Greek Platonists Plotinus, Proclus, and Plutarch—and they got their ideas from Pythagoras and Trismegistus and Zoroaster. Wow!

Ultimately, as you can see, the trajectory of the ideas that "thinking positively creates positive outcomes" and that "thoughts are things" can be traced back through time to the philosophy of such ancient thinkers as the Greek mathematician and philosopher, Pythagoras of Samos; the Egyptian god-king Hermes Trismegistus; the Persian prophet Zoroaster; and even to Babylonian and Akkadian myths! Indeed, we might have to go back beyond written time to find the source of this wisdom!

So, in the twenty-first century, we have taken these ideas, rooted deep in history, and incorporated them into a modern self-development paradigm which teaches that we can reconstruct ourselves by thinking positively—how cool is it that! Our modern pursuits are the same as those of our ancestors from hundreds of centuries past! For the ancients, self-development was a sacred calling, inspired by ethereal gods and guided by myth.

Today, we reconstruct ourselves, we strive to be the best versions of ourselves for both spiritual and secular reasons, and we follow the "positive thinking" model because we know it works. However, while philosophers, self-help gurus, and healers from arcane to modern times have propounded that thinking positively works, they do not tell us *why* or *how*. To find out, we have to look to science, back beyond Greek philosophers, Egyptian sages, and Babylonian mages, to the beginning of time.

Thoughts are Things

As noted, the fundamental concept behind the Law of Manifestation is that *"Thoughts are things."* This profound idea can influence your life in significant ways! As we have seen—and as we will see later in this book—many people today are using this concept to manifest their destiny and change their lives through the power of positive thinking, using positive affirmations. But why do optimistic thoughts and affirmations work so well? It's simple—thinking positively activates a scientific process based upon the operations of quantum physics. *What you think and say out loud puts the creative power of the universe into action.*

The *science of manifestation*—thinking and affirming your way to realizing your dreams —is rarely explained in a manner that can be understood. Sometimes, it seems that it's a secret known only to quantum physicists. But this mystery is worth exploring because understanding it will bring us closer to living the lives we want to live. So, we're going on a little trip—into the quantum universe!

On our journey into the science underlying the effectiveness of positive affirmations, we have to go deep into the past, back beyond recorded time. It is a long journey into this distant past, and to navigate the road ahead, we'll need sacred guides. The guides we will use are the mystical shapes and forms of sacred geometry, the building blocks of life.

Studying sacred geometry proves that thoughts are—and, from the beginning, always have been—things. *So, into the science of sacred geometry we go....*

Sacred geometry combines geometry with a spiritual understanding of the universe and of nature. It reveals the interrelationship between gravity and energy, mass and time—and their effect on the natural and spiritual worlds. In sacred geometry, we find the key to the creation of the universe, the reason why *thoughts are things* and why affirmations, said aloud, are among the most creative forces in the cosmos.

It is said in The Bible that, "In the beginning...the earth was without form and darkness was upon the face of the deep" (Genesis 1:1-2) and that, "In the beginning was the Word and the Word was with God and the Word was God" (John 1:1).

Because the word *God* means so many different things to so many people, for the purposes of this investigation, we'll call the creator "the Divine," and refer to the Divine as both male and female. And we'll keep in mind that another word for "the Divine" is "Love."

Sacred geometers (mathematicians who study geometry) say that this Divine Word, or *Logos*, was the loving source of all creation, and that from the geometrical configuration of the *Logos,* all of creation was realized.

How? The Prime Cause, the vibrating *I Am Love* consciousness that was/is the Divine (the so-called 'Zero Point thought'), wished to know and experience Himself. His loving desire was so great that from out of the nothingness that was the Divine spun a somethingness, an infinite circle of blissful, loving Awareness. And so it was that this circle was imprinted upon the darkness. A single *form* manifested out of the formless void. *Divine thought became a thing.*

When this happened, what was whole became for the first time divided; the Divine thought herself into being! For sacred geometers, this sacred circle was made of light and had the sound of "Aum." That sound was the *Logos—the Word*. So, Divine Love vibrated in the anti-matter of the cosmos, and from Love, a dynamic sound and a particle of light emanated. The vibration caused by the marriage of light and sound projected a second circle upon the void, the so-called *Vesica Pisces ("Veh-si-kah Pisk-kehs")*, one circle overlapping another circle. Thus, from out of a loving thought came the Word and out of the Word the first complex, sacred form emerged!

From out of the *Vesica Pisces* spun all of the sacred geometrical shapes that are the basic building blocks of nature—the Flower of Life, The Fruit of Life, Metatron's Cube, the Phi Spiral, and the Golden Mean Rectangle. The Fibonacci number sequence too, long revered as descriptive of the beauty and proportion in science and nature, is concealed within these geometric configurations. It is beyond the scope of this book to describe the profound metaphysical meanings of these shapes, but suffice it to say that from these quintessential shapes, every known form and substance in our world can be created. And, when you comprehend the secret science that underlies sacred geometry, you can become the creator!

Sacred geometrical shapes are richly symbolic, showing us that everything in the known and unknown universe is interconnected, that every facet of reality spins out of un-reality. The whole is the sum of its dynamic parts, the inner is in balance with the outer, and earth and spirit resonate in oneness. Sacred geometry shows us that the infinite, creative universal mind and the consciousness of humanity are one and the same! In a phrase: *You are God.*

We can use the imagery and symbols of sacred geometry to transcend our limitations, to expand our self-awareness, and to tap into our innate creativity to achieve our dreams. We have only to go within, to a quiet, reflective place and seek—as the Divine did in the beginning—to Love and to Know Ourselves. When we transcend ordinary consciousness, through meditation and self-reflection, we will integrate our deepest strengths and unlock our ability to transform our lives.

Rising to our fullest potential, we will be guided to access the universal love and unity that dwells in us. We must embrace all of who we are, so that we may become our true selves. Then, we will be empowered to access our Divine energy and sacred creativity.

And that is how the science of manifestation works. The Divine's focused, loving intention (desire) became a thought. Divine thought created sound, light, and matter. So, *Love* was First Cause, and *thought* was its effect. Then, *thought* was the cause and *sound and light* were its effects. Then *sound and light* were the cause and *matter* was the effect.

And that process, expressed in very simplified form, is the science you need to know to understand why and how positive thinking and positive affirmations work. *Love (First Cause) is the greatest creative force of the universe.* When Love begets thought, thought begets sound, light, and matter. *When you love, think, and affirm, magic happens!* This is not just an inspirational idea—it's a law of the universe. That's why it is so important not simply to think and affirm, but to *think positively* and *affirm aloud, positively.* Positive thought is loving thought and, ultimately, love is the positive thought form that sparks all of creation—the Divine Love that vibrates through the macrocosm of the universe is also the stuff of which the microcosm of our own world is made.

Remember, you live in the world, and within you lives the light and love of the Divine. So, as you travel on your sacred journey towards personal transformation and self-fulfillment, meditate upon Love. Meditate upon the universal magic that exists within the sacred geometric shapes that are the building blocks of the creative cosmos. Use the images, love, and power that emanate from them to manifest your own dreams. Affirm your hopes and dreams aloud— *and turn your thoughts into things.*

Once you understand these laws, you can apply them, and begin to work with the mechanics of Universal Law to create your own reality. I encourage you to study the early section of this chapter in depth, meditate upon the laws of the universe, and then practice the Twelve Principles outlined below. Take the time to dive into each principle, and deepen your understanding of them. They will change your life!

Here is a wonderful affirmation to help you harness the power of the spoken word...

> Every time you say, "I AM," you are affirming "*God* in me is…." And when you affirm, it is *God* who affirms through you.
>
> I invite you to create your own affirmation (or you can use this one) and confidently claim the *God* force energy within you. Feel the power of *God*/Creation as you speak your affirmation.
>
> *I AM grace, I AM peace, I AM seeking and reaching higher states of being. I AM allowing source energy to flow through me, I AM here to heal, to love, to serve, and to ground a higher vibrational energy for all of humanity. I surrender to the Most High. I invite my angels and guides to walk by my side. I am here to thrive!*

Think Big – Using the Twelve Principles

Before you begin practicing the Twelve Principles outlined below, reflect on what would fulfill you. What inspires you? What would you like to experience in your life? Your grand goal may take some time to surface because often, we have never asked ourselves these questions or allowed ourselves to *Think Big*. But remember, the universe is vast, it has an unlimited well of energy, and there is nothing too big or too small to ask for—the well will never run dry.

As you have seen, nothing is "out there," everything is "right here," within you. This can be hard to believe due to your early conditioning and your brain's way of rationalizing everything. You may be met with some resistance in the beginning of this work—that is normal and expected—you are stretching yourself further than you have ever have before.

To truly access and manifest the life you desire, you must take this practice *seriously*. Remember, your predominant mental state governs the direction of the energy you project. What you think, you create. Imagination is the key to creation, so be sure to take the time to visualize what you want. Think of it, and *feel* what it is like to have it in your reality. This type of reflection anchors your thoughts and emotions deeply and directs your intentions.

Being aware changes everything. Practicing your mindful intentions daily will reprogram your subconscious mind. Start observing your thoughts and notice how you may contradict your intention by thinking the words "can't" or "won't." Remember, we are not defined by nor tied to our circumstances, we are not our past, we are not our future, we are not the projections others have placed upon us. We are entirely who we choose to be, here and now.

When we know this, when we integrate it into our hearts, we can use the Law of Attraction in our favor to manifest all of our desires. But caution is advised here—ask yourself, "What am I focused on?" "Do I want material wealth or spiritual prosperity?" Ultimately, one is a distraction and the other is our salvation. That said, we can have both without restriction if we stay grounded and maintain the clarity that physical gain does not go with us when we are done with this life. True wealth is accumulated through our relationships and through our life experience. We are powerful, and using the tools to access and amplify our power can lead us down a lonely path if we do not first reflect on the true meaning of life and seek balance. When we are spiritually prosperous, when we follow our passion and purpose and live a life of good intentions for all, we naturally attract material wealth and lay the foundation for free-flowing, creative energy to direct all of our earthly affairs.

Consciously harmonizing with the unwavering power of Divine creativity can mean the difference between a life filled with lack, hardship, fear, anxiety, and struggle—or one of joy, satisfaction, limitless prosperity, peace, and fulfillment.

When we create a clear channel of communication with the Divine, we come to trust that everything we need will come to us. We no longer need to know *how* it will come. This is hard for the human mind, as it desires innately to know in detail how everything will work out. This is because most of us were conditioned at an early age to accept that abundance is not our birthright, that in fact, lack is the reality for which we are destined. So, open your heart and free your mind—and trust that all will arrive in Divine time! And, when you are manifesting your heart's desires, just remember to *Think Big!*

Trust the Universe

When we are open and trust that the universe is on our side, we are in alignment and we become magnets for the manifestation of our intentions. The most important facet of this process is to be grounded in gratitude for all that you already have—because simply existing at all is a miracle.

To raise your vibration and set the tone and foundation to step into your role as a powerful, conscious creator, it helps to practice awareness and mindfulness daily. As you become consciously aware of your thoughts, as you shift them towards your intentions, you step into the space of creation. Engaging your imagination and concentration, and following up with action is the power behind manifestation. When we act as if we already have everything, when we are open to receive gratefully, the universe miraculously provides abundantly far beyond our limited human understanding. As noted, this is not magic—it is a *law*.

As noted earlier, the Divine energy of the cosmos runs through every fiber of your being. When you open your heart and mind to your cosmic connection, you realize that you are a direct reflection of Divinity, a unique expression of All That Is And Ever Has Been.

The twelve universal laws are as real as the laws of physics and they govern your life—whether you realize it or not, or want them to or not! We live within a sea of cosmic energy, with unlimited potential to create our own reality.

The Law of Divine Oneness (Immutable)

All life, all energy comes from one source. We all come from the same source, we are all connected, we are all living expressions of the Divine. We must learn to recognize the Divinity that is within all things and respect it. You are not a tiny, insignificant drop in a vast ocean. Those who see themselves as "small" send out vibrational energies that are also "small." You are a part of an energy source that is so vast and immeasurable that the mind cannot comprehend it. Your goal is to learn to see the ocean within the drop.

This is why it is important for us to learn unconditional love, because when we hurt another, we are hurting ourselves—as we are a united, universal family. Whatever action you take, whatever thoughts you think, and whatever words you speak directly impact the harmonious state of the All. The macro-universe is a living organism. It constantly receives and gives energy, it constantly creates material reality. When we decide to contribute to it positively, we are "in the flow" and are showered with blessings and support for our grander vision of life. Synchronicities flow. The right people and events come and help us to move forward in becoming who we want to be and experiencing what we want to experience.

The Law of Vibration (Immutable)

"Nothing rests; everything moves; everything vibrates." According to a famous Hermetic text called *The Kybalion* (see below), everything in the Universe moves, vibrates, and travels in circular patterns; the same principles of vibration that exist in the physical world apply to our thoughts, feelings, desires, and wills in the etheric world. Each sound and thing, and every thought has its own unique vibrational frequency.

The Law of Vibration states that each thing in the universe, seen or unseen, when broken down into and analyzed in its purest and most basic form, consists of pure energy or light which resonates and exists as a vibratory frequency or pattern. The Law of Vibration tells us that we must align our energy with what we want to attract. We do this through the power of our thoughts and emotions, which we can choose to redirect at any moment. Combined, thoughts and feelings comprise a powerful energy that activates the creative power of the universe. So, choose your thoughts and feelings wisely!

When you find out what you want, allow your discovery to instill feelings of enthusiasm and joy within you. This in turn will give you energy to move in the direction of your dreams. These feelings are the ones you need to take action on. When you act as if what you desire is already in your possession, you align yourself with the vibrational frequency of that which you desire—and bring it into manifestation faster.

You must truly act as if you are what you WANT to be—in order to align your energy with that and help it manifest. Not fully recognizing this law is why the Law of Attraction fails miserably for many people. So, if something irritates you—bless it for teaching you a lesson in spiritual wisdom, let it go, and jump back into your feelings of enthusiasm and joy. Remember, in order to materialize your desires (energy frequencies) in the physical world, you must match the frequency you want to attract into your life with a similar thought, feeling, word, or action. That is why the Law of Vibration is also called the "Act *As If* Law."

If, for example, your goal is to attract wealth, you need to act as if you already possess wealth. You must focus on the feeling that wealth would bring you, *feel* the joy of it being created in the non-physical realm, and trust your *knowing* that wealth is coming to you. You don't need to worry about how it will happen or become entangled in the details. Your only job is to stay focused on good feelings around your wealth, and to raise your vibration around the concept of wealth. The truth is that whatever you want is already created for you—it is already present in the Universe! All you need to do is align with that vibration and allow it into your life.

The Law of Action (Immutable)

In order for us to manifest things on this physical plane we call Earth, we must employ the Law of Action. That is, we must engage in actions that support our thoughts, dreams, emotions, and words, for the power behind manifestation is, firstly, our imagination; secondly, our concentration; and thirdly, our action. We cannot expect things to fall into our laps without intentional effort, without moving the energy and putting our ideas into action.

But you may ask, "Why do I have to struggle?" You don't! If you are "struggling" to reach your goals, it means you are not properly aligned with them, or they are not the right goals for you. Hard work—when it is something you are passionate about—should be challenging, but it should also come easily to you. This is where most of us fail—we might know what we want but we fail to take action. We might be skeptical, feel unworthy, or not feel capable of achieving our dreams. Perhaps we see limitations or no way out, perhaps we are depressed or exhausted from living in harsh conditions. But we must banish these doubts and limiting thoughts and take inspired actions every day that help us move towards our goals. Do not, however, take radical jumps into the unknown, for that can cause lower-vibrational emotions of stress and fear, which in turn will only create resistance in the natural flow. Focus instead on what makes you happy and grateful, keep your vibration up, and follow signs that guide you to your desired experience. Take steps towards your goal daily, always keep the energy in motion—no act is too small—and stay focused on your goals.

The Law of Correspondence (Immutable)

"As above, so below." This law states that just as the quantum mechanics of our vast universe are reflected in the workings of the smallest quark, your outer world reflects also your inner world. Simply stated, you are destined to experience what you think about—and your world reflects this to you, every day. If you want to change external circumstances in your life, you must change your inner world first; those who seek inner peace find that their life runs more harmoniously overall. They are better able to cope with life's little upheavals and carry on while still holding an attitude of appreciation and gratitude. Those who get stuck in anger, resentment, and other self-sabotaging emotions and beliefs, however, find that they tend to draw more chaos into their lives—and likely, they don't even realize they are doing it. Truly, we have to clean up the disharmony within ourselves in order to align with the perfect harmony of the universe.

It is the disharmony of our self-limiting beliefs that keeps us from feeling worthy or capable. We must love ourselves first, the rest will follow. If we don't belief in ourselves, the universe is going to going to respond to how we feel. Remember: you are far more powerful than you may know, you just have to remember this, and truly *feel it* to claim your birthright. *It has to start with you.*

The Law of Cause and Effect

"You reap what you sow." *The Kybalion* states this law thus: "Every Cause has its Effect; every Effect has its Cause; everything happens according to Law; chance is but a name for Law not recognized; there are many planes of causation, but nothing escapes the Law."

This law, also referred to as "Sowing and Reaping" or "Karma," states that any action produces or returns a result or outcome in exact proportion to the act or cause which initiated it. To simplify: *what you do comes back to you*. Many spiritual traditions have taught this universal wisdom in various ways. If you are passionate and driven in positive ways, for example, you will put forth powerful energy and actions that will return to you in the form of rewards. On the other hand, if you are negative or hurtful towards yourself or others, the consequences will be visited upon you. We must take full responsibility for our actions and accept the karmic consequences that come to us from this lifetime—and from other lifetimes. (*Please see the section on Karma for more information on this law.*)

The Law of Compensation

This Universal Law says, essentially, that the result of the Law of Cause and Effect is that the visible effects of our deeds are given to us in gifts, money, inheritances, friendships, and blessings—in essence, the law states that abundance is provided to us.

So, get better at what you are doing, study in your field of interest, always continue to seek and reach for higher understandings and offerings. You will always get back what you give to others. There is a saying that "misery loves company." When you are miserable, you attract other people who are also miserable, and it becomes a vicious cycle. Fortunately, the opposite is also true! If you want to receive more of something in your life; *be what you want to see*. Give freely to others what you hope to receive. "Does this mean," you might ask, "that if I need more money I should throw away the money I have?" No, but you should be generous and share abundance according to your capacity to do so. Provide for those who are in need by giving of yourself. Be generous and share abundance in its many forms with others—and abundance and prosperity will return to you. The Universe returns like for like—and that means that we are free to send out what we want in order to receive more of it.

The Law of Attraction

This Law demonstrates how we create the things, events, and people that come into our lives. Our thoughts, feelings, words, and actions produce energies which in turn attract like energies. *Like attracts like.* Negative energies attract negative energies and positive energies attract positive energies. This is why it is important to focus on manifesting positive energy through the use of the various laws of the universe. It goes beyond merely "wishing," "hoping," or "visualizing" as many New Thought teachers suggest. If you want to attract positive energy—you have to line up with it and apply yourself to attracting it. You cannot change the world, but you can change your perception about the world and all around you will change, because when you vibrate on a positive note you can attract only "like" energies.

The Law of Attraction ensures that whatever energy you broadcast out into the universe is joined by (or attracted to) energies that are of an equal or harmonious frequency, resonance, or vibration. (Please see the chapter on the Law of Attraction, where we delve more deeply into this topic.)

The Law of Perpetual Transmutation of Energy

All persons have within them the power to change the conditions of their lives. Higher vibrations consume and transform lower vibrations; thus, each of us can change the energies in our lives by understanding the Universal Laws and applying their principles in such a way as to effect change. As we have seen, energy is in constant motion and all energy eventually manifests in physical form. This Law also states that you have the power to change your life. Higher vibrational energies consume lower energies, so if you don't like the path you are on, change it—or, more importantly—"allow it" to be changed.

Rather than try to "force your will" on people or on circumstances, rearrange the way you think and choose to empower yourself. Go with the flow. When we resist change, or try to assert a false sense of control over the external world, it always leads to struggle. Struggle leads to resistance. The ego's need for a false sense of control can block the flow of positive energy that will bring the ideal circumstances you are searching for to you. Fear-based thinking can undermine your progress in all areas if you don't recognize it. So, embrace change, work with these cosmic energies, and "allow" circumstances, opportunities, etc. to manifest in your life according to Divine law.

The Law of Relativity

This Law states that each person will receive a series of problems (tests of Initiation/Lessons) for the purpose of strengthening the light within them. These tests/lessons challenge us to remain connected to our hearts when we are solving them. This Law also teaches us to compare our problems to others' problems and to place them in proper perspective. In other words, no matter how bad we perceive our situations to be, there is always someone who is in a worse position. In other words, "it's all relative," and "it is what it is." Nothing is good, bad, big, or small, etc. until it has been experienced and compared to something else.

This Law teaches that every soul will face challenges, and it's what you do with those challenges that define you and determine what you become. You can remain under pressure or rise above it and allow your trials to strengthen you. Learn to use your life's challenges as stepping stones rather than seeing them as stumbling blocks. Keep things in perspective. Seek all the "blessings in disguise" that surround you. We all have the power to make ourselves miserable and weak or happy and strong. The amount of energy required for these opposites is the same—the choice is yours.

The Law of Polarity

This Law states that, "everything is dual; everything has poles; everything has its pair of opposites; like and unlike are the same; opposites are identical in nature, but different in degree; extremes meet; all truths are but half-truths; all paradoxes may be reconciled." (*Kybalion*)

Do you ever wonder why, in a world of unfathomable abundance, we must sometimes go through events, conditions, or circumstances that we perceive as unpleasant? Becoming aware of and developing a deeper understanding concerning the Law of Polarity may provide the insight you need. All things have an opposite—day and night, masculine and feminine, joy and sorrow, dark and light, hot and cold, male and female. Without one, the other could not exist.

Thoughts and ideas that are not working for your highest good can be removed by consciously directing your attention to their opposite. Feeling sad? Watch a funny movie or play music. Feeling angry? Rather than dwell on that emotion, focus on what you can do to manifest its opposite. In this way, you find solutions that are both inspiring and empowering. *God*/Source has created everything, including things we perceive to be "good" and "bad." It is not our place to judge. We must remain neutral, and understand that everything in creation has an equal and opposite side, that everything serves us as a force of spiritual evolution and expansion.

The Law of Rhythm

This Law states that all energy vibrates and moves according to its own rhythm. These rhythms establish cycles and patterns. Think of the seasons, for example, which form a full year. Each season has its own purpose and function, but is a vital part of the full circle.

Learn to harmonize with the higher vibrational energies that you seek to attract. Raise your vibration through the understanding and practice of the other universal laws, and harmonize with those higher energies.

Many people use Meditation to connect their energy to source energy and, as a result, they maintain "higher frequencies" and a sense of connection throughout each day. They know that, as *The Kybalion* says, "Everything flows, out and in; everything has its tides; all things rise and fall."

Spiritual and Ascended Masters know how to rise above negative parts of a cycle by never getting too excited and never allowing negative things to penetrate their consciousness. What happens in your outside circumstances is not important until you respond to it. You can choose to "ride the wave" and trust that "all is well," or you can resist, fight against, and prolong the negative condition. Everything has a meaning and a purpose in your world and the sooner you understand and accept that, the sooner you will understand that there are no coincidences, there are only synchronicities meant to bring you closer to your desires and to who you truly are.

The Law of Gender

This Law states that all things have both masculine and feminine energies—yin and yang.

The union of these yin and yang principles gives birth to everything in creation. In order to grow, all things require space, time, and nurturing.

All things need a period of gestation and growth before reaching maturity; our task is to balance the masculine and feminine energies within us, achieve Self-Mastery, and become co-creators with Universal Consciousness.

Above, in the section on the Laws, we mentioned an arcane text, *The Kybalion*. A study of the Hermetic philosophies of Ancient Egypt and the ancient Near East, *The Kybalion* is based on mystical teachings attributed to the Egyptian god-king, Hermes Trismegistus. It is of interest to note that Hermes Trismegistus, like his Greek/Roman counterpart Hermes Mercury, did not actually exist. His "teachings" are a compilation of various ancient Egyptian philosophers and sacred scribes of late antiquity and attributed to Hermes Trismegistus, the so-called "Thrice Great," because he is said to have invented mathematics, literature, and science. Also attributed to Hermes are the practices of art, magic, law, medicine, philosophy, and countless others. Hermes is also associated with the Egyptian god, Thoth.

The Kybalion was written by three anonymous philosophers calling themselves the "Three Initiates," who claim that their book reflects the core teachings of Hermes the Thrice-Great. They claim that there are *Seven Hermetic Principles* upon which the entire Hermetic Philosophy is based. It is no mistake that some of these seven principles are included in the *Universal Laws* noted above. Whether there are "seven ruling principles" or "twelve universal laws" which guide our lives will remain a debate for scholars and seekers for eons to come. According to the authors of *The Kybalion*, the seven principles are:

1. THE PRINCIPLE OF MENTALISM
   "The All Is Mind; The Universe is Mental."

2. THE PRINCIPLE OF CORRESPONDENCE
   "As above, so below; as below, so above."

3. THE PRINCIPLE OF VIBRATION
   Nothing rests; everything moves; everything vibrates."

4. THE PRINCIPLE OF POLARITY
   "Everything is dual; everything has poles; everything has its pair of opposites; like and unlike are the same; opposites are identical in nature, but different in degree; extremes meet; all truths are but half-truths; all paradoxes may be reconciled."

5. THE PRINCIPLE OF RHYTHM
   "Everything flows, out and in; everything has its tides; all things rise and fall; the pendulum-swing manifests in everything; the measure of the swing to the right is the measure of the swing to the left; rhythm compensates."

6. THE PRINCIPLE OF CAUSE AND EFFECT
   "Every Cause has its Effect; every Effect has its Cause; everything happens according to Law; Chance is but a name for Law not recognized; there are many planes of causation, but nothing escapes the Law."

7. THE PRINCIPLE OF GENDER
   "Gender is in everything; everything has its Masculine and Feminine Principles; Gender manifests on all planes."

These principles are powerful realizations! Once we begin consciously to navigate our own thoughts and emotions in the direction of our intentions, we realize that our energy flows where our attention goes. What an incredible lesson, what a wonderful life tool to learn, practice, and teach! As it says in *The Kybalion*: "The Principles of Truth are Seven; he who knows these, understandingly, possesses the Magic Key before whose touch all the Doors of the Temple fly open." And, as the Three Initiates say: "He who grasps the truth of the Mental Nature of the Universe is well advanced on The Path to Mastery."

Taking Action – Putting the Laws and the Science to Work for You

The power of positive thinking has been front and center in the media for several years. As noted earlier, numerous modern authors and thinkers write about the power of intent, propounding that there is a secret to manifestation that involves thinking positively and tapping into the so-called "Law of Attraction." Maybe you've read all the books, applied yourself to focused intending and thinking positively—and maybe all you've attracted to yourself is a pile of bills for too many books and online courses. Maybe it hasn't worked for you. Maybe you have given up.

But, do not dismay. There really is something to the power of intention, the law of attraction, the secret of manifestation, and the potential of positive thinking. The thing is, it's not wholly about intending, it's also about desiring, loving, and accepting. It's about getting all of you involved in the process—you can't just *think* your way positively to manifesting your dreams, your whole mind, body, and soul have to be engaged.

Once you understand how the process works, you realize that manifesting what you want isn't a secret—it's a science. Once you understand how the mechanics of the universe work, you'll have everything you can think, feel, and love your way to.

We talked about the phrase, "As Above, So Below." To reiterate, what this means is that for everything in the created universe (the macrocosm), there is an equivalent thing that is small (the microcosm). As we have seen, all of the cosmos was at one time a great void, filled with potentiality. In the darkness of space, something infinitely small was waiting to be created out of the vastness of nothing. It's a complex concept, but it's also simple.

In the beginning of time, nothing existed. All the finite shapes, structures, and properties of a finite world lay superimposed as potentialities upon an infinite, loving universe: substance and form were floating nebulously upon formless, non-substance. Then, from the depths of this darkness, the Divine creator became aware of her loving self, she desired to manifest herself, so she began, as is the Divine's nature, to create.

From the core of the cosmos, a spark of Divine creativity radiated outwards and burst forth in a Big Bang, or *fiat*. And the form of the fiat was a multi-dimensional fractal of energy; a simple, tiny circle recreated itself, moving infinitely outwards in every direction, all at once, in one immeasurable fraction of a millisecond, and the universe and everything in it was born.

So, that's the science that underlies the creative mysteries of the universe and *it's the science you must understand and use to manifest your best reality*. It is as we have seen written in *The Kybalion*, reflecting the words of Hermes Trismegistus: *What is in the greater is in the lesser. What is in the macrocosm is in the microcosm. What is above is also below. What is universal is individual*—in a phrase, what is in Divine-Love-stuff is in *you*.

What does this mean? In the simplest of terms, it means that you are—we all are—*a creative piece of the Divine*. You can seize this creative power to create the life you want through directing your mind, body, and soul towards purposeful, active, positive thinking.

It means that we all possess an innate ability to create whatever we desire. We can do this by applying the laws of physics, of mathematics, and of consciousness to our thoughts, senses, and emotions. Like the Divine in the beginning—who thought himself/herself/itself into existence, *what we think we can create.*

It means that the principal elements of our physical world: earth, air, fire, water, and ether, are the loving energy of universal conscious thought expressed in material form. They are the building blocks we can use to create material things. Just as every known shape and form in our physical universe is created out of that first shapeless and formless void—out of Love, thought, and desire—just as we are created beings, we are also creative.

Amazing science, right? We are fragmented pieces of the Divine, multi-dimensional entities trapped in a dimensional universe; spiritual beings living in a material world, powerful beyond measure. But we have forgotten how to tap into our Love and our power and regain union with our Divine, creative source.

To remember our capacity to create, to remain in balance with the spiritual here in the world of physical form, and to become who we truly are, we need to embrace the truth—we are the creators of our own realities! We are made of Love; the spark of Divine creativity dwells within us. Our mind's thoughts, our physical senses, and our heartfelt emotions are the building blocks we can use to create whatever it is we truly desire.

But how do we do it? Here's a true story about how it works. Feeling alone one winter's day, and remembering the creative force within, a friend of mine decided she would manifest a passion flower. She got herself in a better mood by doing some vigorous exercise, and envisioned a passion flower. She thought about how much she loved this flower's exotic bloom, how wonderful she always felt when she could enjoy one. She made the imagined passion flower as real as possible in her mind, saw it, felt its waxy petals, smelled its honey-sweet perfume, heard bees buzzing around its vine, tasted its sticky nectar. Then, she floated a technicolor, holographic image of it out of her conscious mind and imprinted the image upon the ether. She said aloud, with as much love as she could muster, "Today, I will see a beautiful passion flower." She released the image and went back to her day.

Now, recall that it was mid-winter, with several feet of snow on the ground—and that passion flowers bloom in summer. My friend had no plans to go out that day, so it was an impossible request she had made of the universe. But, about an hour later, she heard something come through the mail slot, and she picked it up. It was a garden maintenance company flier for spring garden clean-up. The front cover photo—a beautiful passion flower!

Her heart soared when she saw that passion flower. Her mind felt sharp, clear, and alert. She felt all her senses come alive as she was reminded in that ecstatic moment that we truly are creative beings. With the power of our minds, and the workings of our five senses, we have the power to create whatever we can hold in our loving thoughts. It is really as though we can reach into another dimension and pluck out the thing we want!

On another occasion, feeling blue and wanting to be assured that her angels were near, this same friend asked to manifest the impossible—a white elephant. About two hours after thinking, sensing, and loving the idea of having a white elephant, she went out shopping. As she got in her car, she stepped on something. It was a tiny white elephant, about ½" long, carved of ivory. She carried this ivory elephant with her for fifteen years, a daily reminder that we humans are creative entities.

Notice that my friend did not ask for a *live* passion flower or a *living* white elephant—it's daunting to think of what might have happened had she remembered to add that feature to her manifestation process!

Now, remember, some things might take longer to manifest than others—a passion flower or a white elephant might take less time than a house, for example. But the concept of time does not exist beyond our world of time and space. In the netherworld, where creativity and creation begins, all time is *now*. It is just a matter

Aligning with the Divine

of *really visualizing* the thing that you desire in your mind, *really loving* that thing with all your heart and soul, imagining it as a three-dimensional object and experiencing it, allowing your body to come alive with sensation, feeling it with all your senses. Then, it is a matter of releasing it and trusting that the universe will send it to you.

But—and please read these next sentences as if they appear on a flashing neon sign in letters two feet high—*You have to keep your spirits up, love the object of your desire fully, keep a detailed representation of it in your mind, keep it viscerally experienced in your senses, and remain open to receiving it. If you allow yourself to doubt, to have misgivings, or to question the universe's timing (e.g. saying, "It's been three days and it's not here yet!")—then it is not likely the thing you desire is going to appear.*

Did the Creator doubt when the universe was unfolding? No—there was just the loving desire to know and experience Self. Everything that happened after that was a natural evolution of that loving desire.

Becoming a good manifester takes practice. You can't run a marathon on your first day on the track, and you can't likely manifest a Ferrari or your dream job on your first try. So, to manifest what you desire, start small—and practice.

Remember—simple "positive thinking" isn't the beginning and end of the process of manifestation. As noted earlier, you have to get your body, mind, and soul involved. Your body's five senses have to be completely invested—see, hear, feel, smell, taste—*viscerally*. Your mind has to concentrate intensely on creating concise, focused thoughts of the thing you desire—and the pictures it creates for you need to be specific and clear. Your soul—and by "soul" in this context I mean "heart"—has to be pure, vibrant, and brimming with love for the thing you desire and for all of humanity. And, your heart has to be filled with gratitude for the things you already have now—and one of those things is the thing you desire. That's right—and this bears repeating—you must embrace the fact that the thing you want is *already yours.*

By nature of being human, you already have the power to turn your positive thinking into positive manifesting. Put these positive thinking secrets to work for you and you'll manifest your dreams. It's so simple. You are a creative being, mind, body, and soul!

> *Your beliefs become your thoughts,*
> *Your thoughts become your words,*
> *Your words become your actions,*
> *Your actions become your habits,*
> *Your habits become your values,*
> *Your values become your destiny.*
> —Mahatma Gandhi

3

Earth - The Cosmic College

> "A human being is a part of the whole...(and)... part limited in time and space. He experiences himself...as something separated from the rest, a kind of optical delusion of his consciousness. This delusion is a kind of prison for us, restricting us to our personal desires and to affection for a few persons nearest to us. Our task must be to free ourselves from this prison by widening our circle of compassion to embrace all living creatures and the whole of nature in its beauty."
> —Albert Einstein

How would your life change if you believed that life on earth is a school for your soul's evolution and that you—in your physical body—are a student in this school of life? What if, by being here, your soul is assuming a role in the ever-expanding consciousness of creation itself? What if the goal of everyone who incarnates on Earth is enlightenment and ascension into Divinity? And, what if, in the end, we are all unique expressions of Divinity having an amazing human experience?

I believe that the response to all of these *What if* questions can only be: "It's true!"

When we arrive on this earth plane, we are pure Source energy / Divine creative energy / the Prime Mover incarnated in physical bodies. We are, in a word *God*—or whatever name you wish to call the great creator of all things. An incorporeal, nether-worldly energy has come to earth to experience life in a corporeal form. As *God*-energy on a journey of exploration, we are here on a mission—to experience life in the physical world. Our greatest aim is to expand our souls.

In each lifetime in this physical world, our unique stream of consciousness that is Source/*God* energy (i.e., our individual soul) abides within a human physical body. As we cross the threshold from the non-physical nether realms into the physical world at birth, our souls forget their spiritual source and who they truly are. This is imperative so that we can become fully present in the physical, three-dimensional realm. Only by forgetting who we truly are— eternal, Divine beings—will our souls have the greatest potential of mastering the balance of polarity and duality here on the earth plane. Were we able to remember our spiritual selves and our Divine lives on the other side easily, we would all be flocking like lemmings to the nearest cliff—because Earth School is sometimes too hard to bear and, if we could, we'd all make our way home immediately.

So, while for the purposes of the soul's growth it is desirable not to remember our lives at home in the spirit world, it can also work the other way. So, it is paradoxical: it is easy to fall into the trap of believing that life here in the corporeal world is all there is, and we can fail to learn life's valuable lessons simply because we lack the awareness that we have intentionally incarnated to learn.

In a way, it is as if our souls come to the physical world to play a game of self-mastery, while simultaneously assisting in the evolution of the human race, and raising the level of human consciousness.

When our game is done, and our human bodies die, our souls find their way back to their home to the world of spirit—where their accomplishments are celebrated by the soul families who know how difficult it is to be at "Earth School."

As our souls journey into the plane of matter in each human lifetime, we are offered opportunities to undergo unique experiences that are vital to our soul's expansion. Just as on earth, a baby must grow into a child, into an adolescent, and into an adult, in the spirit realm there are also infant souls, toddler souls, teen souls, adult souls, and old souls. In each lifetime, each type of soul chooses to become strong and empowered, and thereby learn its lessons—or unhappy and weak, and thereby live life avoiding its lessons in this incarnation. It is up to each soul whether or not to awaken in this physical realm—and if the soul chooses simply to enjoy the physical experience of being on the earth plane, then its lessons can wait until its next incarnation. The soul alone is 'in charge' of its own progress—and if it chooses to remain in Grade 1 for eternity, that's okay! Most souls, however, actively seek expansion. So, they descend down through the Divine light into the plane of matter and density to experience separation from the Divine as well as the many facets of human emotion that they cannot feel in the spirit world.

Walking in earth's gravity is a huge challenge for the soul, as the low, dense energies on earth are difficult to navigate compared to the higher-vibrational realms our souls are used to moving in. We each incarnate from pure source energy, the highest vibration of All That Is. We each come from perfection to experience imperfection—and when our lives are over, we rise again to Divine perfection. Over the course of many soul journeys and many incarnations, we will each fully master the polarities offered here on earth. Being mindful and aware helps us to direct our energies towards our intentions—which, as noted, are to grow, experience, and expand into Divine awareness.

In order to learn and grow, before we incarnate we choose the people in our soul groups with whom we make what are known in the New Thought movement as "soul contracts"—pre-agreed experiences and events that will assist both us and them in mastering our lessons. Those lessons are frequently about love and forgiveness. The souls and the experiences we choose are catalysts for triggering us into feeling and facing emotions that will serve our evolutionary process. Thus, our earth families, friends, lovers, co-workers—even strangers with whom we experience significant life events—are all mirrors for our soul's expansion.

Being in Earth School is surely a challenge for the higher vibrational soul, but be that as it may, all is as it is designed to be. Your soul/energy is a gift to the ever-expanding consciousness of creation. You are at the forefront of All That Is; and the Divine knows itself through you and your experiences. You are a direct reflection of the ALL; you are a unique expression of Divinity; and you are valuable to creation itself, for you *are* creation itself.

So, whether we are aware of it or not, we human beings are all here on the physical plane to experience spiritual growth, to expand our personal consciousness, and to expand the consciousness of the collective. As developing souls, we have all had many past incarnations/lives. Each lifetime was a part of our soul's evolution and we each continue to return to earth to complete our lessons and to clear our karma so that we can move on to a new space of exploration in the creative, cosmic process. Just as children on earth must start in kindergarten and graduate Grade 12 by passing all of the grades in between, our souls must also learn spiritual lessons, and, as each lesson is learned, our vibration is raised and we vibrate more closely in tandem with the godhead.

Remember, spirituality is not something you seek. You are spirituality itself—a spirit experiencing physicality. We are both the students of life and the teachers of its lessons. So, are you ready? School's in session!

Spiritual awakening is not one moment in a person's life; awakening is a life-long journey of falling away from the illusion of our separation. Aspects of ourselves die as we evolve spiritually—when we release what does not serve our highest good, we create space for more profound and beautiful human experiences. This can be a painful process as your soul stretches. These are growing pains—they are temporary. Remember, *what we resist persists*. When we look at what life is showing us, when we bring our shadows into the light and integrate them, we find balance and harmony.

> "Everything in existence is our teacher—if we are open to perceive it and then receive it."
> —Chantelle Renee

Karma – Stepping out of the Karmic Cycle

> "Our greatest teachers are the reflections we refuse to look at."
> —Chantelle Renee

So, what is karma? Karma is the Law of Cause and Effect. The concept derives from the early Hindu text, the Rigveda. Karma is a fundamental doctrine of Buddhism and other ancient wisdom teachings. The doctrine of karma existed for fifteen hundred years before the birth of Christianity and we find reference to it in The Bible: "As a man soweth, so shall he reap" (Galatians 6:7-9). Karma can be thought of as "energy/consciousness in action."

The Law of Karma states, in essence, that every thought, word, feeling, action, and intention that you send out into the universe will return to you. The Law of Karma is also called the Universal Law of Cause and Effect, which we discussed earlier. Thus, every action (including our thoughts) has a reaction or consequence. We do indeed reap what we sow. So, choose your thoughts and your actions wisely—you are in constant conversation with the universe! Nothing in your life occurs by chance or by mistake—everything acts according to Universal Laws.

The Law of Karma is exact. Whatever energy is sent out goes around, gathers momentum, and returns back to the sender either as positive or negative karma. Sometimes the return of karma is instantaneous but not always. Some of us are dealing with karma from yesterday, others of us are dealing with karma created lifetimes ago.

This Law of Cause and Effect is not punishment, but instead it brings us situations and circumstances that will produce lessons for the sake of the soul's education. Awareness of your current and past life karma gives you great power, for as you take responsibility for your own actions, thoughts, and intentions, you can balance karma much faster.

Focusing upon service to others can be a great karma balancer. One cannot serve with the intent of balancing one's karma, however, one must serve from the heart, with integrity, with the intent of assisting others to reach their highest potential and to feel unconditional love.

Aligning with the Divine

Another way of balancing any negative karma we may have consciously or unconsciously created is through the path of initiation. Everyone is being initiated at all times in all moments—by our freely-made choices, we are constantly allowing source energy to work in tandem with us for our good—or we are resisting source energy. When we resist, our past karma creates blockages in our auric field, tying up our light and energy, and affecting both our perception about life and our ability to manifest our desires and live the lives we are truly meant to live. Earth truly is the cosmic college for evolving souls—and karma is its greatest teacher. Our souls must balance, transmute, and integrate all karmic lessons—that is life's ultimate test.

But who is giving our souls these tests? Sometimes it is our Higher Self, compelling us to deal with situations we have been neglecting or trying to avoid. At other times, it is an Ascended Master providing lessons our souls are ready to learn. The master's purpose is to test and strengthen our soul and to help us learn to be virtuous in all our dealings. It is important to remember, however, that we are never given more than we can handle and that the purpose of any test is to help us make progress on our spiritual path, and to help us to heal.

Spiritual growth and healing go hand in hand. Many of the initiations we receive have to do with balancing karma, with improving our well-being on a psychological level, as well as with healing our inner child (soul). Most of us are carrying around emotional baggage—not just from this lifetime but also from previous lifetimes.

It is no good trying to avoid your karma or to blame others for any life challenge you face or any predicament you may find yourself in. Playing the victim role does not serve you. You came to live in this physical world in order to balance and master your karma, and to expand your soul. So, embrace every problem that comes your way and handle it sincerely and with love. Confidently bring forth your best thoughts and intentions around finding a solution. Hold a non-judgmental attitude and be willing to discern what is really important to your spiritual growth and what is not. Become the observer of your life, and always observe without judging. Remember too, always extend forgiveness to yourself and to others in every difficult situation. This is the path to balancing your karma, expanding your soul, and transcending the human condition.

Releasing Karmic Bonds

Karma pushes and pulls us until we transcend it; it continuously creates new opportunities for us to master each of our lessons. Its energy is a catalyst, prompting us to become more present and aware. If we view our karmic lessons as blessings, they can motivate us to extend forgiveness instead of blame, to practice kindness rather than cruelty, and to cultivate compassion in the face of aggression. Our karmic blessings—if we can accept and resolve them—can impel us to surrender to spirit with gratitude, thereby reclaiming our spiritual gifts and reuniting with spirit.

If you are ready to resolve your karma and to step forward onto the path of self-empowerment, I invite you to speak your power into existence. Here is an affirmation you can use—or, you can create your own.

> *I choose to release my karma, to evolve past my limitations, and to forgive all who have trespassed against me. I choose love and faith over fear and hate. I am ready to participate in co-creating heaven on earth. I take full responsibility for the energy I give as well as the energy I receive. I am loved unconditionally*

and I love others unconditionally. I choose to break the chains that have kept me in the energetic tide of resistance. I am free to expand. I am ready! I am the master of my own reality!

4

Energy Awareness

> "As we explore the aura and the chakras, it is important for us to view our journey not as revolutionary, but rather as very traditional. Chakras, as well as auras and electromagnetic fields, are as old as the earth itself. The chakra system, in fact, is a part of the ancient and lost mysteries. And, in the end, the chakra system in our bodies is how we find our way back to the most ancient mystery of all—God, the Oneness, the Omniscient."
> —Rosalyn L. Bruyere, *Wheels of Light*

To gain self-mastery, to consciously co-create with *God*, and to work in tandem with creation itself, we must shed the karmic bonds we have acquired—in this lifetime and in other lifetimes. We must let go of the limiting beliefs and actions that are rooted in our karmic lessons, and in turn, free ourselves to connect into higher vibrational states of being. To do this, it is helpful to understand the universal energetic forces that underlie the very dynamics of life.

Universal Energy

We are subject to universal energy and we all move with the energetic rhythms of nature. Through the seven vortices of the *chakras*, and through the seven planes of the subtle body or *aura*, cosmic energy moves downward, from spirit into form, and outward, from matter into spirit. The energy of the chakra system draws life-force into our bodies and animates us. Everything in the natural world is fed by this universal energy.

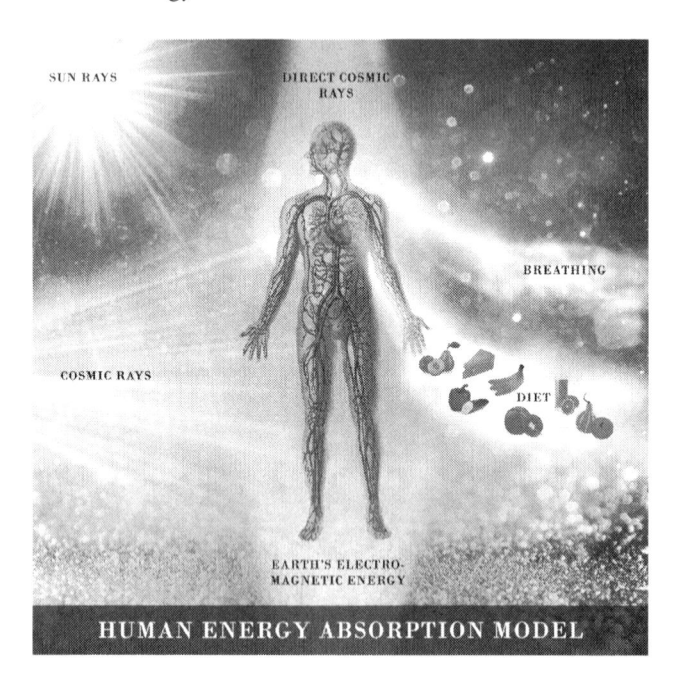

HUMAN ENERGY ABSORPTION MODEL

As we move through the world, the energy we exchange with others and with our environment is gathered up and absorbed into our auric fields. It is through this vibrational relationship, between body and spirit, mind and matter, and heaven and earth, that we live and have our beings. Our physical health as well as our spiritual wellness depend upon the power and vitality of our energy systems, for we are connected through our subtle energy systems to the intelligence of the universe—in a phrase, we are united with one another and with the cosmos through our bodies of light!

The Torus

> "Above all else, guard your heart, for everything you do flows from it."
> —Proverbs 4:23

Before we delve into what it means to have an energetic body—or "light body," it is important to understand that we are all part of an energetic whole that reaches to the end of our known universe and beyond. Our limited physical bodies exist inside a subtle, invisible—yet powerful—energy field that moves in sync with the energy of the universe. Our energy body exists within the core of what is known as the *torus*.

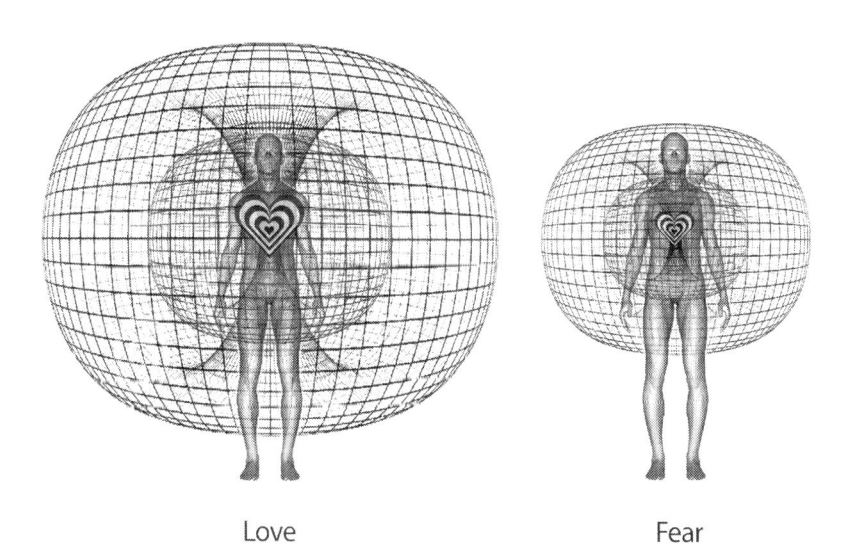

Love   Fear

In geometry, a torus (plural *tori*) is "...a surface of revolution generated by revolving a circle in

three-dimensional space about an axis coplanar with the circle. If the axis of revolution does not touch the circle, the surface has a ring shape and is called a torus of revolution."
—Wikipedia

The torus is a self-regulating system that exists in practically all forms of creation from animals, humans, atoms, cells, seeds, flowers, fruits, trees, hurricanes, planets, suns, galaxies, and the cosmos—just to name a few! The torus is a self-sustaining, powerful magnetic field; it has its own time and space and corresponds with the unseen energy field around us.

We can imagine the torus as a doughnut or bagel. The holes at the top and bottom allow us to connect intimately to the universe and others around us. The torus field surrounding each human being allows us to experience our uniqueness and differences while simultaneously being "one" within the quantum field. Thus, we have *the illusion of separation* and, through our distinctive experiences, we can expand spiritually.

Being aware of your toroidal flow helps to keep your energy flowing freely and keeps you tuned into and connected to your environment. Energetically, it also allows us as healers to give and receive energy without restriction.

The toroidal flow also shows us that the more harmonious a human being is, the more harmonious humanity as whole will become. This is not just wishful thinking—it is physics. Unified, our hearts are incredibly powerful.

The human heart is the electromagnetic generator of your individual energy field. Living a life fueled by love, passion, and joy will surely create a high-vibrational toroidal flow. Divine energy surrounds us at all times, why not open your heart and invite it in?

Love   Love

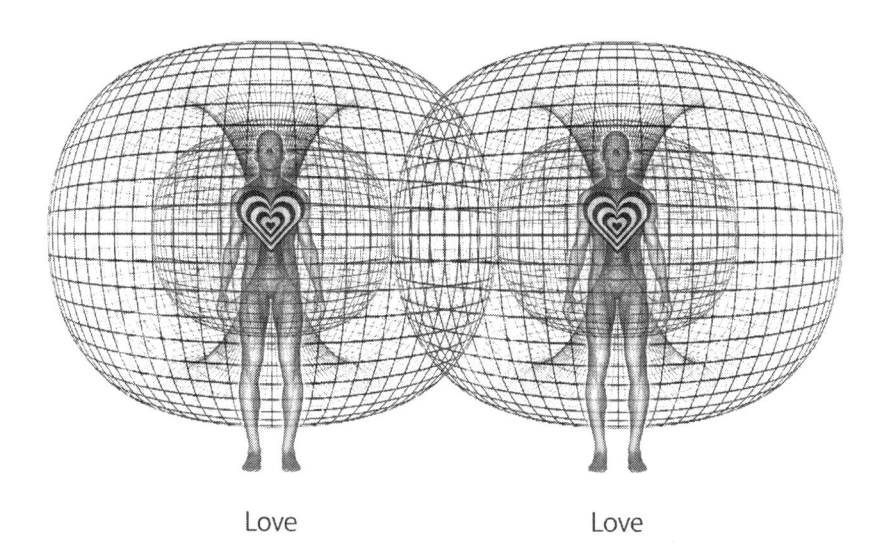

It is important to reclaim your own energy and direct it consciously. As we clean up the disharmony within ourselves, we can align to the perfect harmonics of the universe. As we become still in our centers and still within our minds, our loving hearts will beat as one with the universal mind.

> *Every living being is an engine geared to the wheelwork of the universe. Though seemingly affected only by its immediate surrounding, the sphere of external influence extends to infinite distance.*
> —*Nikola Tesla*

Cymatics – The Science of Frequency

> "Energy cannot be created or destroyed, it can only be changed from one form to another."
> —Albert Einstein

As we become conscious of our energetic bodies and our oneness with all things, we begin to realize that everything—and that means *everything*—in the universe is made up of waves and particles. And these waves and particles manifest in myriad forms—as solid things we call *matter*, and as *light* and *sound*. Depending on a variety of factors too complex to delve into here, waves, light, and sound are constantly shaping and re-shaping themselves into every known form in our physical universe.

The study of wave phenomena and the ability of sound to organize and restructure matter is called *Cymatics*. This study shows us how frequencies of sound waves manifest as perceivable matter, ultimately making sound visible.

The term *cymatics* was coined by Prof. Hans Jenny, a Swiss scientist and Anthroposophist (1904-1972). Professor Jenny found in his research experiments that sound waves passed through different kinds of impressionable matter—such as water or sand—caused the formation of geometric patterns.

In order to explore wave phenomena, Jenny created an acoustic device called a *tonoscope* that used crystal oscillators to allow viewers to see beautiful and detailed patterns created by sounds. Jenny found that patterns formed by matter subjected to high-pitched frequencies were complex, harmonious, geometrical, and symmetrical while less complex and disharmonious shapes formed when matter was exposed to lower frequencies.

Since these experiments prove that sound influences matter in this profound way, can we surmise that cymatic patterns are continuously unfolding throughout the Universe? And, does Jenny's cymatics experiment prove the theory we have propounded about the creative energy of sound? As we noted earlier, in John 1:1 in the New Testament it says, "In the beginning was the Word, and the Word was with God, and the Word was God." In the ancient Hindu Rigveda, we read, "In the beginning was Brahman with whom was the Word, and the Word was verily Brahman." Indeed, these sacred texts lead us to the conclusion that sound (the Word) was (and is!) the driving force of creation.

And, if the sacred words in the Rigveda and the Bible are not enough to convince us, we can turn to the words of one of the greatest scientists of all time, Nikola Tesla, whose words provide concrete evidence that sound and vibration are creative forces: "If you want to find the secrets of the universe," Tesla said, "think in terms of energy, frequency and vibration." Science and religion express it differently, but the meaning is the same: sound and vibration are the secret creative forces in the universe.

Tesla and Jenny are not the only scientists to suggest that sound has super powers! Other researchers have done similar experiments to Jenny's and have made astounding discoveries. For example, Japanese author and researcher, Dr. Masaru Emoto, has done experiments on water which have proven that sound, words, and even thoughts can create miraculous changes in the molecular structure of water.

As the human body is made up of more than 50% water, it stands to reason that we are influenced by sound and thought waves! Most of us are not aware of the direct impact that frequencies have on our minds, and on our emotional, physical, and spiritual states. The truth is that sound creates a visible and dynamic geometrical pattern in every water molecule and cell in our bodies.

The impact of sound on our physical body and energy system is substantial.

Dr. Emoto's water images are truly beautiful and inspiring. They prove that matter is inherently responsive to sound and intention! They remind us that we are part of a complex, intricate vibrational matrix and that we possess far more control over our vibrational states than we previously believed.

The insights of researchers like Emoto, Tesla, and Jenny can inspire us to remain always in flow with the laws of the universe so that we may consciously and harmoniously co-create with nature. Think, for example, about the power of such simple acts as remaining in gratitude and blessing our food or water before consuming it. With our loving thoughts and good intentions, we can transform the very cellular structure of matter! Similarly, when we say "thank you" and "I love you," or we send out caring thoughts to those in need, we are using the science of sound and vibration to harness our Divine powers of creativity. As Dr. Emoto says, his experiments are "The power of love and gratitude made visible."

> "When you have become the embodiment of gratitude, think about how pure the water that fills your body will be. When this happens, you yourself will be a beautiful shining crystal of light."
> —Masaru Emoto - *Messages from Water*

Remember, it's up to you utilize the energy of sound and vibration in your own life. Why not start with blessing your water each day? Write love notes to the water you bathe in, water your plants with, and consume. Before you drink a glass of water, say "thank you," bless it, and confirm that it is sending healing, harmonious energy to every cell in your body. Start small—harmonize your water, harmonize your life!

Dr. Jenny's and Dr. Emoto's findings help us to remember that we truly are one with the Divine and that we are powerful beyond measure. Their experiments empower us to take full ownership of the sacred temples of our bodies and minds and to begin consciously to choose what vibration we want to reside within.

Energy Anatomy – The Subtle Body

What is a subtle body? What is an aura? What is a chakra? These are words healers and metaphysicians use to describe aspects of the energy systems of the human body (in energy medicine the physical body is called the "gross body"). Imagine an egg-shaped field of light extending two to three feet outward from your physical body, surrounding and permeating your whole being. This subtle body of spectrum light is called the "energy field," "subtle body," or "aura."

With practice, you can learn to see this energy field and use its colors and vibrational patterns to identify congestion or blockages in the energy field which may lead to the compromised well-being of your friends, family, and clients.

The Aura

AN INTRODUCTION TO THE HUMAN AURA ENERGY LAYERS

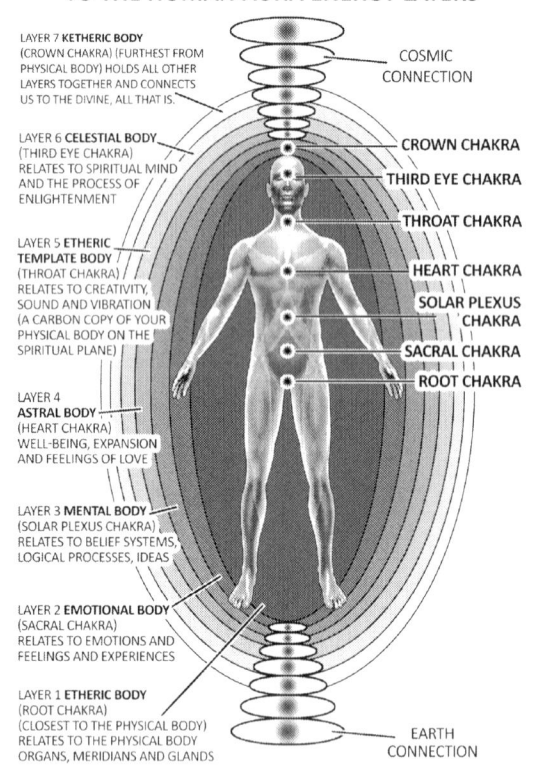

LAYER 7 **KETHERIC BODY** (CROWN CHAKRA) (FURTHEST FROM PHYSICAL BODY) HOLDS ALL OTHER LAYERS TOGETHER AND CONNECTS US TO THE DIVINE, ALL THAT IS.

LAYER 6 **CELESTIAL BODY** (THIRD EYE CHAKRA) RELATES TO SPIRITUAL MIND AND THE PROCESS OF ENLIGHTENMENT

LAYER 5 **ETHERIC TEMPLATE BODY** (THROAT CHAKRA) RELATES TO CREATIVITY, SOUND AND VIBRATION (A CARBON COPY OF YOUR PHYSICAL BODY ON THE SPIRITUAL PLANE)

LAYER 4 **ASTRAL BODY** (HEART CHAKRA) WELL-BEING, EXPANSION AND FEELINGS OF LOVE

LAYER 3 **MENTAL BODY** (SOLAR PLEXUS CHAKRA) RELATES TO BELIEF SYSTEMS, LOGICAL PROCESSES, IDEAS

LAYER 2 **EMOTIONAL BODY** (SACRAL CHAKRA) RELATES TO EMOTIONS AND FEELINGS AND EXPERIENCES

LAYER 1 **ETHERIC BODY** (ROOT CHAKRA) (CLOSEST TO THE PHYSICAL BODY) RELATES TO THE PHYSICAL BODY ORGANS, MERIDIANS AND GLANDS

COSMIC CONNECTION

CROWN CHAKRA
THIRD EYE CHAKRA
THROAT CHAKRA
HEART CHAKRA
SOLAR PLEXUS CHAKRA
SACRAL CHAKRA
ROOT CHAKRA

EARTH CONNECTION

It is believed that the aura is fashioned in a sort of hierarchy of light, with each plane (or layer) being built upon the one 'above' it. It is imagined as being made up of between five to seven energetic layers, each one vibrating at a different frequency and being a different color and intensity of light. The densest layer (called the etheric body) lies next to the gross body and pulses at the slowest rate.

As the aura's layers blossom outwards, they become progressively more refined. Thus, the furthest layer from the body, the causal body (often called the ketheric body), is the lightest and vibrates at the fastest rate. The aura's "subtle bodies" are broken into three classifications, from the bottom to the top of the human body. All of these bodies are named, and the names vary depending upon which spiritual or healing tradition you adhere to. We will name them all here, from the innermost layer to the outermost. (Further research will assist you in deciding which names or systems resonate with you and work most effectively in your healing or metaphysical modality.) The bodies are:

- *Three bodies exist in our physical plane*; these conduct physical-world energies and are named the etheric (vital), emotional, and mental bodies;
- The *astral body* is said to mediate between the physical and spiritual bodies; and
- *Three spiritual bodies* connect us to the higher, cosmic realms: spiritual (etheric template), celestial, and causal (ketheric).

It is important to know that these bodies are not separate one from the other, for as we move from the innermost planes to the outermost, each contains the vibrational stuff of the field before it. Hence, the causal body contains all the qualities of all the other energetic bodies. Then, extending even further out from the light body are the cosmic bodies (called the monadic, buddhic and atmic), which mediate between the universal consciousness and the spiritual realm. (As the cosmic bodies comprise a system too complex to discuss in brief, please feel free to research these on your own).

Each energy field is associated with an energetic or electromagnetic frequency, a musical note, a color, and each has an emotional, mental, spiritual, or physical attribute. Each plane is also said to contain its own seven-part chakra field, which processes the spectrum of light rays and sound frequencies resonating within the field. Hence, you can see already with our simple diagram that we can calculate forty-nine separate chakras (7 subtle energy fields x 7 chakras in each = 49)—and that's just the beginning of this complicated energetic system! As noted, we'll keep it simple and only deal with the seven major chakras.

So, imagine! As we move through the world, we are bodies of light, spinning like whirlwinds, connecting and disconnecting with others, in a dazzling kaleidoscopic of color and a euphony of sound!

The Seven Major Chakras – Part I – Alignment to Source Energy

> "If your eye be single; your whole body shall be full of light."
> —Matthew 6:22

The chakras are sacred energy centers located along the spinal column which play a major role in our overall health and vitality. Chakra means "wheel" or "disc" in Sanskrit and the chakras are so-named because these energy systems spin like vortices outward from the spine to the fronts and the backs of our bodies. You can imagine each of the seven major chakras as a funnel-shaped, whirling mass of energy, in which a mild suction operates (like a whirlpool), drawing universal energy down into the physical plane and into the body. In the chakra system, each vortex contains (among other energetic patterns) programmed or imprinted energy that governs our experience. We draw to ourselves the energy that we vibrate in harmony with—and that's all the more reason to get our energy systems balanced so that we can create a lighter, happier experience here on the physical plane! Having a healthy chakra system is key to living a successful, abundant life.

The chakra system originated in India between 1500 and 500 BCE in a large body of ancient sacred texts called The Vedas. According to traditional teachings, there are over 88,000 chakras in our beings. In more recent belief systems, there are primary and secondary chakra systems and channels through which our *chi* or *prana*—also called *vital energy* or *kundalini energy*—flows (*see also below*). These channels are also called *nadis*—and there are as few as 114 or as many as 72,000 of these channels in our physical bodies—depending upon the belief system you work with. As noted, in this section, we will discuss just the seven main chakras in the human body and the effect they have on our consciousness.

The seven major chakras are, starting from the ground up:

- The root chakra, located between the legs in the area of the perineum,
- The sacral chakra, located above the pubic bone, below the navel,
- The solar plexus chakra, located in the area of the navel, below the breast bone,
- The heart chakra, located center-chest, in the area of the heart,
- The throat chakra, located at the center of the throat,
- The third eye chakra, located between the eyebrows,
- The crown chakra, located at the top of the head.

Please refer to Part II, below, to learn specifics about each chakra, which body part or emotion it relates to, etc. and how the health / balance of each chakra can affect our lives. For now, suffice it to say these wheels of light are the catalysts of consciousness and govern our basic human functions. They control everything from our survival instincts and self-esteem to our ability to communicate and experience love freely.

As mentioned, each chakra relates to certain organs, glands, and life issues. If one or more chakras are blocked, restricting the flow of source-energy, we may experience emotional and health problems and an overall feeling of stagnation. Physical and emotional traumas create pain and result in a negative energetic charge in the associated chakra. Limited energy flowing in the chakra system can also prevent us from obtaining higher states of consciousness.

If you envision your chakras as pools of energy that vibrate within the subtle body—the etheric, astral, and mental planes—you can begin to appreciate that if your pools of light become stagnant with stress, poor diet, and the simple trials and tribulations of everyday life, you can prevent energy from flowing freely, thus creating disharmony within your being.

Holistic practitioners believe that many of our physical ailments are rooted in an imbalance of our emotional, physical, spiritual, mental, or subtle bodies. Illness may be caused by a blockage in energy flow through the chakras, or may be due to a disturbance in our subtle light body.

The light body, being connected as it is to universal intelligence, knows how to heal itself. Our job as healers—and as 'owners' of bodies—is to listen to the wisdom of the light body, to balance the chakras, the aura, and our subtle energy bodies, and thereby to aid in the rebuilding of the mind-body-spirit connection and the recovery of vibrant health. Our bodies speak to us in the language of light—we simply need to learn a new way to listen.

The Seven Major Chakras – Part II – Healing with the Chakras

Many people do not know about the incredible life-force energy and healing power that lies within each and every one of us. Our subtle energy centers—our auras and our chakras—govern our experience on the earth plane, they connect us to the unseen cosmic sea of energy that surrounds us at all times.

Our auras are, in a sense, treasure chests containing gifts of higher senses just waiting to be accessed and unlocked. For example, the seven major chakras within the aura are said to be in direct communication with seven rays of cosmic light and, connected together, they create the so-called "rainbow bridge"—a celestial link that allows cosmic energy to flow continuously from us to Spirit and our higher Selves, filling our bodies, minds, and souls with the light of the Divine. This energy flows in and out and is absorbed and processed through each chakra. Thus, our chakras are the streams of energy that flow from our physical body to the spiritual, heavenly bodies.

At the base chakra is a powerful energy called kundalini energy (also known as 'serpent energy'). When this sleeping, spiritual energy is awakened, it rises up along the spine and through each chakra, activating its full potential. As each chakra is returned to harmony within itself, a process is activated whereby an energy vortex is opened and the perfected qualities and energy of that chakra are projected upward into the next chakra. The process is repeated until the crown chakra is activated. As we raise and stabilize this kundalini energy, we reach a state of energetic harmony and begin to create our own reality consciously. The chakra system begins to spin at such a high revolutionary rate that it turns the spinal column into a blazing pole of light and the Rays of the Creator pour down through the pole of light and infuse all of the chakras.

As our chakras awaken, they start to spin. The light emanating from them resembles a lotus flower unfolding its petals, opening up to the light. This is why each chakra is symbolized by a many-petaled lotus flower. Each chakra also has a unique color—and combined, their colors manifest as the human aura.

Below, we present an overview of the meaning, function, features, and purpose of each of the chakras in the human subtle energy field. As you begin to work with the chakras, try to connect with each center; use the mantras and the gems associated with each one to aid you in opening to the flow of energy through that chakra. For example, sounds create vibrations in the body to help your cells to work in harmony. Chanting the tones or sounds affiliated with each chakra will help to align the chakras and heal the parts of the body related to that chakra's energy. Similarly, placing gems and semi-precious stones strategically during meditation and visualization can assist in balancing the chakras.

The 1st Chakra – the Root Chakra (Muladhara)

1st MULADHARA (Root chakra)

This symbol represents the four-petaled lotus. The word Muladhara breaks down into two Sanskrit words: Mula meaning "root" and Adhara, which means "support" or "base."

- Color – Red.
- Element – Earth.
- Location – Base of the spine, the first three vertebrae, the pelvic floor.
- Body Connections – Skeleton, spinal column, leg, foot, blood, bone, teeth, rectum, immune system, adrenal gland.
- Mantra – "LAM."
- Gems – Black tourmaline, bloodstone, garnet, red jasper, hematite.
- Represents – Security, safety, survival, basic needs (such as food, sleep, and shelter), physicality, physical identity, grounding.
- Life Lesson to Master – The Muladhara chakra asks us to find safety and security while residing in the physical plane, to satisfy our basic needs for survival, and to embrace belonging to both the microcosm and the macrocosm.
- Indications – The root chakra is where we ground ourselves into the earth and anchor our energy in the manifested world.
- Symptoms which indicate the root chakra is out of balance or that its polarities are either overactive or underactive include lack of self-esteem, procrastination, low sex drive, materialism, selfishness, egotism, a dominating personality, being overly-focused on sexuality, being possessive, or being fearful. People who are excessively negative or cynical, who

have eating disorders, who are greedy or avaricious, who feel unfocused or ungrounded, who are always in "survival mode mentality," who are frequently victimized, or who are homeless may be suffering from an imbalance of root chakra energy.
- Symptoms that indicate the root chakra is harmonious energetically include feeling grounded and safe, having free-flowing energy and the ability to manifest abundance easily, being self-aware and having conquered the ego, and having entered the realm of self-mastery.
- Circumstances which contribute to root chakra trauma include experiencing a difficult childhood, lacking a bonded relationship with the mother, enduring physical abuse or abandonment, living in an unsafe or fearful environment, or living in an oppressive or controlling religious belief system.

The 2nd Chakra – the Sacral Chakra (Svadhisthana)

2nd SWADHISTHANA (Sacral chakra)

This symbol represents the six-petaled lotus. The word Svadhisthana can be translated as "the dwelling place of the self."

- Color – Orange.
- Element – Water.
- Location – Lower abdomen, one to two inches from the navel.
- Body Connection – Ovaries, testes, womb, kidneys, bladder, mid-spine.
- Mantra – "VAM."
- Gems – Amber, orange calcite, carnelian, hematite, citrine.

- Represents – Emotions, relationships, sexuality, sensual pleasure, feeling the outer and inner worlds, creativity, imagination.
- Life Lesson to Master – The sacral chakra offers us the opportunity to express our creativity freely, to be fully, unconditionally present with our emotions, and to maintain our own identity and strength when engaging in activities and behaviors with others.
- Indications – Symptoms that the sacral chakra is out of balance or that its polarities are overactive or underactive include having feelings of guilt, sexual shame, sexual dysfunction, resentfulness, or shyness. This person may fear change, be depressed, be dependent or codependent, be submissive, self-serving, manipulative, volatile, or aggressive. An individual with an unbalanced sacral chakra may see others as sexual objects, may be controlling or lustful, and may have sexual obsessions or even a lack of sexual desire. They can have addictive personalities, may overindulge in fantasies, may be driven by their emotions (or may stuff their emotions), and/or they may feel numb or disconnected.
- Symptoms that indicate the sacral chakra is energetically in harmony include possessing strong intuitive skills, and being kind, friendly, and caring towards others. This person is in tune with their emotions and is creative. They experience a sense of wellness, and enjoy an abundant, pleasurable, and joyful lifestyle.
- Actions and situations which can result in trauma to the sacral chakra include sexual, emotional, or spiritual abuse, neglect, denial of a child's feelings, living in an alcoholic or drug-addicted family, or living with a family that engages in religious extremism.

The 3rd Chakra – the Solar Plexus Chakra (Manipura)

3rd MANIPURA (Solar plexus chakra)

This symbol represents a ten-petaled lotus. The word Manipura means "lustrous gem."

- Color – Yellow.
- Element – Fire.
- Location – Around the navel, in the area up to the breastbone. The solar plexus chakra is a source of personal power. It governs self-esteem, the power of transformation, and warrior energy.
- Body Connections – Pancreas, stomach, liver, gallbladder, spleen, small intestine, upper abdomen, digestion, blood sugar, eyes, feet.
- Mantra – "RAM."
- Gems – Citrine, golden topaz, amber, apatite, aquamarine, aragonite.
- Represents – Personal identity, personality, confidence, self-discipline. This chakra governs the ability to take responsibility for one's life and one's intellectual and mental abilities. In balance, the Manipura chakra helps a person to shape their personal opinions and beliefs, and to make confident decisions. It controls a person's will, personal power, and independence.
- Life Lesson to Master – The solar plexus chakra helps us to live our life's purpose without fear, judgement, or the need to manipulate or control others, and aids us in the quest to know who we are, at our core.
- Indications – Symptoms which indicate the solar plexus chakra is out of balance or that its polarities are overactive

or underactive include being deficient in personal power/energy, lacking purpose or ambition, misusing power or being manipulative, and/or wielding excessive control or authority over an environment or over others. The individual with an out of balance Manipura chakra may experience insecurity, self-consciousness, or low self-worth. They may be overly sensitive, may cast themselves in the role of "servant," and may be obsessed with pleasing others. This person may be a workaholic and may not feel comfortable with authority figures—yet may be irresponsible. Or, they may be overly ambitious or have a superiority complex. They may be obsessed with minor details, may 'overthink' things, and may frequently feel confused, helpless, or overwhelmed.

- If a person's sacral chakra is harmonious energetically, they will feel relaxed, self-confident, and joyful, and will possess strong personal power.
- Situations and conditions which will cause trauma to the solar plexus chakra include living in a controlling relationship, having excessive responsibilities, enduring physical or emotional abuse, and being bullied.

The 4th Chakra – the Heart Chakra (Anahata)

4th ANAHATA (Heart chakra)

This symbol represents a twelve-petaled lotus. The Sanskrit word for the fourth chakra is Anahata, which means "unstruck" or "unhurt."

- Color – Green.
- Element – Air.
- Location – Center of the chest.
- Body Connections – Thymus gland, heart, cardiac plexus, breasts,

lungs, diaphragm, lymphatic system, circulatory system, and blood.
- Mantra – "YUM."
- Gems – Emerald, malachite, jade, rose quartz, clear quartz, green calcite.
- Represents – Love for oneself and others, relationships, compassion, empathy, forgiveness, acceptance, transformation, change, and the ability to grieve and reach peace. The Anahata chakra is our center of awareness; it controls our ability to integrate spiritual insights. This is the area where physical and spiritual realities meet; the bridge between our earthly and spiritual aspirations, our energetic connection with the All. In this heart-centered place, we can love unconditionally, and can appreciate the beauty in all things.
- Life Lesson to Master – To experience a true, Divine connection between yourself and others; to give and receive love freely.
- Indications – Symptoms which indicate the heart chakra is out of balance or that either of its polarities are overactive or underactive include feeling as though one is unloved, and feeling victimized, indecisive, stressed, or jealous. This person may be unable to feel—or, on the opposite side, may be paranoid, heartless, or ruthless. They may have a fear of intimacy but also be afraid to let go. They may be codependent, may rely on others' approval, and may try at all costs to please others. They may even take on the role of 'savior' or 'rescuer.' On the other side of things, however, they may be antisocial and isolate themselves, they may be closed down emotionally—or they may express their emotions inappropriately. They may be manic-depressive, experience mood swings, be overly defensive, hold a grudge easily, or have difficulty forgiving others.

- When a person's heart chakra is in harmony energetically, they feel unconditionally loving, compassionate, empathic, and are balanced emotionally. It is through this chakra that we may transcend our personal identity and the limitations of the ego, and experience deep, meaningful relationships.
- A heart chakra can be traumatized if a person experiences abandonment; physical, emotional, or sexual abuse; the death of a loved one; a divorce; grief; or betrayal.

The 5th Chakra – the Throat Chakra (Vishuddha)

5th VISHUDDHA (Throat chakra)

This symbol represents the sixteen-petaled lotus. The Sanskrit word for the fifth chakra is Vishuddha, which means "especially pure."

- Color – Blue.
- Element – Ether.
- Location – The throat.
- Body Connection – Thyroid, parathyroid, jaw, mouth, tongue, larynx, throat, trachea, esophagus, neck, neck vertebrae, ears.
- Mantra – "HUM."
- Gems – Sapphire, blue topaz, lapis lazuli, aquamarine, turquoise, amazonite.
- Represents – The Vishuddha chakra relates to the element of sound. Through it, we speak, listen, and express ourselves. This is the chakra of communication, whether verbal or non-verbal, external or internal, on the physical plane or in the etheric realms. Our intuitive abilities as well as our creative skills are exercised through this energetic center.

Through the throat chakra, we project our ideas outward, we realize our true purpose in life, and we speak our truth.
- Life Lesson to Master – To be heard and understood, and to speak effectively and authentically.
- Indications – Symptoms which indicate the throat chakra is out of balance or that its polarities are overactive or underactive include being self-righteous, arrogant, egotistical, forceful with one's opinions, controlling, judgmental, manipulative, unreliable, or cowardly. An individual with an unbalanced throat chakra may lie, gossip, talk too much or inappropriately, or may make hurtful comments about others. They may speak in a weak or small voice, be excessively shy, be fearful of speaking (or of speaking their truth), be unable to express their thoughts coherently, be unable to listen to others, or they may talk over others. They may lack communication skills, be unable to receive intuitive guidance, be unable to keep secrets or to keep their word, or have no connection with their life's purpose.
- An individual whose throat chakra is in harmony energetically is a centered and clear communicator; they are artistic, compassionate, and can experience Divine energy easily.
- Circumstances that can traumatize the throat chakra include being in an environment with constant yelling or fighting, experiencing intense criticism, not speaking up when required, living in a controlling environment, enduring verbal abuse, or living in a family with an addictive family member.

The 6th Chakra – the Third Eye Chakra (Anja)

6th AJNA
(Third eye chakra)

This symbol represents two elements frequently associated with wisdom—the upside-down triangle and the lotus flower. The Sanskrit word Anja means "command," "summon," and "perceive."

- Color – Indigo.
- Element – Light.
- Location – The area of the "third eye," located in the space between the eyebrows.
- Body Connections – Head, the lower part of the brain, pituitary gland, eyes, sinuses, nose, and face.
- Mantra – "SHAM."
- Gems – Amethyst, lapis lazuli, azurite.
- Represents – Inner vision, deep insight, intuition, movements of energy, perception of the subtle dimensions, and psychic abilities related to clairvoyance and clairaudience. This chakra motivates and inspires our creativity and is the center through which we transcend duality, access mystical states, connect to Divine wisdom, and engage with the realm of spirits and the archetypal dimensions.
- Life Lesson to Master – To trust your insight and intuition (instead of the judgement that arises from holding onto limited beliefs) and to find peace in your own "knowing."
- Indications – Symptoms that suggest the third eye chakra is out of balance or that either of its polarities are overactive or underactive include being egotistical, manipulative, arrogant, dogmatic, insensitive, or oversensitive. The person with an out of balance Anja chakra puts others down, is afraid of success, has an overly analytical mind,

and is limited by fear-based beliefs. They may be meek, undisciplined, or deluded, have a poor memory, unclear thoughts, or a limited imagination. They may live in an illusory reality, demonstrate obsessive behavior, or indulge in fantasies or illusions. They may live in denial of reality and feel stuck in their daily life.
- An individual whose third eye chakra is in harmony energetically trusts their "inner knowingness." They are spiritually aware, imaginative, and tuned into their intuition. They have reached a level of self-mastery and have a pure vision of their life's purpose. They are wise, non-materialistic, charismatic, and they easily manifest abundance.
- The following situations can cause trauma to the brow chakra: invalidation of one's intuition, emotions, or feelings; living in an unsafe or fearful environment; or experiencing oppressive or controlling religious beliefs.

The 7th Chakra – the Crown Chakra (Sahasrāra)

7th SAHASRARA (The Crown chakra)

This symbol represents the thousand-petaled lotus. The Sanskrit word Sahasrāra, means "thousand-petaled." Some describe this chakra as the gateway to the cosmic self; the Divine self; or universal consciousness. It is linked to the infinite, universal mind.

- Color – White, violet, gold.
- Element – Spirit.
- Location – Top of the head.
- Body Connections – Upper brain, pineal gland, right eye, top of the head, midline above the ears, nervous system.

- Mantra – The universal sound of "OM."
- Gems – Amethyst, selenite, sugilite, diamond, clear quartz.
- Represents – Awareness of cosmic consciousness, consciousness itself, communion with higher states of consciousness, connection with the formless, self-realization, liberation from limiting patterns and beliefs, wisdom, ecstasy, and bliss. The Sahasrāra chakra signifies the highest level of consciousness and enlightenment. It is the connective center to spirit; the "focal point" which integrates all the chakras with their respective qualities.
- By mastering the lower vibrational aspects of our beings, we reside in full awareness that we are spiritual beings living a human existence. The crown chakra is associated with the transcendence of human limitations, whether personal or bound to space and time.
- As we are immersed in crown chakra energy, we feel blissfully united with All That Is. This chakra allows us to access to our highest clarity and to attain enlightened wisdom.
- Life Lesson to Master – To experience our full, Divine connection and to know the meaning of life.
- Indications – Signs that the crown chakra is out of balance or that its polarities are either overactive or underactive include feeling frustrated, hopeless, indecisive, or sad. This individual may experience migraines, exhibit manic behavior, or be highly unfocused. They may feel disconnected from spirit—or, on the other side, they may have an obsessive attachment to spiritual matters. They may feel disconnected from their body or from earthly matters, may be isolated from others, or, on the opposite end of the scale, may be caught up in this-world, ego-driven activities. They may be closed-minded, lack imagination, and may feel frustrated that they are unable to realize their true power or attain their goals.

- When an individual is living in harmony with the energy of their crown chakra, they are open to the Divine and are often revered as miracle-workers and highly evolved people—even as real-life alchemists. They have no fear of death for they are self-realized and know that death does not exist.
- Trauma to the crown chakra can arise when a person is forced to live with "borrowed beliefs" or is obligated to participate in religious activities that do not resonate with their true belief systems.

To heal all wounds, we must first calm the war within by allowing light to enter through the lens of awareness. As we create space for more light to enter our energetic bodies, we light up the shadowy places that once kept us anchored in fear and ignorance. We become cosmically aware, we see truly, and are resurrected.
—Chantelle Renee

Spirit Manifested in the Material World

"Everything changes when you start to emit your own frequency rather than absorbing the frequencies around you, when you start imprinting your intent on the universe rather than receiving an imprint from existence."
—Barbara Marciniak

As we have seen, there is an unlimited, unbound well of Divine Source energy that surrounds us at all times. As spiritual beings living in the material world, sometimes we can misunderstand and or misdirect our energetic power. Physical-world challenges, such as unconscious emotional blocks, can lead us away from our spiritual

Aligning with the Divine

path and keep our energies focused on physical-plane issues. Ideally, our mission here is to master our thoughts, energy, and emotions, and to reach full alignment with our souls and with creation itself. By being mindful of the energy we are receiving from others—as well as the energy we are projecting out towards others—we can become energy-aware. This awareness is key—both to walking a path of mastery and to living a life of peace and harmony.

When we are babies, we are like little "love magnets." We attract love easily, and we give love without restriction. Before we are incarnated, we are Divine love and Divine light, untarnished by outside influences, but as we grow up, every hurtful comment or negative emotion that comes our way chips away at us. Those shards of hurt sit in our energy fields—and we tuck them away in our subconscious minds. As this pile of fragments grows, it nourishes itself by attracting more of the same emotions. Thus, over time and experience, we amass a collection of negative experiences in our auras, and we accumulate negative energies in our subconscious minds. Though it lives outside of our conscious awareness, the pain, hate, hurt, and other 'lower vibration' emotions we experience over our lifetimes continue to affect all areas of our lives unconsciously.

Many of us don't want to feel these lower vibration emotions; they remind us of the love we lack. So, we push them away, we don't deal with them. But it is imperative that we do not deny these emotions, instead we must address them as they arise, we must *be present* with them. It's far less painful to address these emotions in the moment than it is to allow them to collect more negative energy that is sure to cause chaos in your life. Remember, negative energies are here to guide us—not enslave us. But we can only learn from them if we embrace them.

Sadly, not only do most of us not deal with our accumulation of unconscious emotions, we let them rule us—and weaken us. Like vampires, they pull our life force energy from us and use it to motivate us in ways that we may not even be aware of. We allow them to foster emotional conflicts between us and others, and then we allow them to draw in others' energies to shore up even more negative-energy resources. It is as if our unconscious emotions take on a life of their own! Over our lifetimes, we develop so many blocks and piles of hurt and pain, and we suppress our sense of higher awareness so often that we do not even realize that these unconscious blocks of pain are hurting us—and everyone around us. Because we crave energy to heal ourselves, and because the energy our vampires draw to us serves us, 'borrowing' others' energies soon becomes a habit. We become dependent upon the attention and kindness of others to keep ourselves motivated and inspired.

But it does not need to be this way. If you look around you, you will realize that your world is replete with energy vampires. And you will realize that you too can sometimes be an energy vampire. In our relationships—with friends, family, colleagues, co-workers, bosses, teachers, lovers, perfect strangers—we pull energy from others. Others also pull energy from us.

But with awareness, we can start to fill ourselves from the inside out, expanding our own inner energy, instead of stealing and depleting others' energy. When we become strong in ourselves, we can stabilize our energy field and stop others from draining our energy. But this only becomes possible when we become aware of the negative energy blockages we have developed over our lifetimes, and when we heal and transcend them. Once we have done this, we can embrace a new method of being in the world—vibrant and energetically whole, we can begin to relate to the world around us with the same love and compassion we had when we were innocent children.

But tapping into this new way of being in the world can be challenging. We have, by and large, all been raised in a spiritually misguided society—instead of filling ourselves from the inside out, we have been taught to seek outside ourselves for our power. This can leave us fragmented, anchored in a lower vibration, and feeling disempowered physically and emotionally. We must take responsibly for our own well-being and stop taking our power from others—and handing our power over to others. This new way of being may be difficult but it is necessary—creating your own reality without getting lost in others' frequencies is the path to self-mastery.

Once we begin to master our own energy and overcome our own vampirism, we have to heal our energy systems. In order to take control of your own energy, you must be conscious of how your energy becomes dissipated. First and foremost, become aware of those others in your environment who may be feeding on your energy—the so-called 'energy vampires.' As noted, they use the light and energy of others to strengthen their own depleted energetic systems. Their efforts are usually unsystematic, random—they'll draw energy from anyone at any time. Energy vampires are usually spiritually immature. Their intentions are most often not malevolent; they pull energy from others simply because they do not realize that they have the same well of abundance to tap into as their victims do.

Energy vampires are not aware that they are actually seeking their own free-flowing energy from their own soul, their own universal connection. If they were able to tap into the energy of their soul, they would be in a state of full awareness and empowerment, open to receive Divine energy freely and abundantly. Instead, like parasites, they feed on others' energy, they crave attention. Because they long for love and affection, but do not know how to fill themselves up with the love within themselves, they anchor their 'needy cords' into your auric field and slowly suck your life force away.

Energy vampires are especially attracted by lower-vibrational human emotions, which activate their need to feed on others' energies. Jealousy, for example, is misdirected admiration and feeling jealous keeps a person in a state of lack and resistance, seeking outwardly for their security, unaware and unable to realize that what they are looking for is within themselves. So—be cautious—when energy vampires seek your attention or your emotional reaction, check in with yourself. Are you feeling strong and positive? Or, are you putting out a lower-emotion vibration, giving an energy vampire the negative energy he or she wants? Are you feeding the energy vampires in your life?

You'll know you're feeding an energy vampire when you become energetically exhausted—it can feel at times like you are walking through life in quicksand, in a constant state of resistance. To support your own expansion and spiritual strength, it's important when you find yourself in this compromised state to look within. Right now, what are you thinking, projecting, and receiving?

We attract energy vampires into our lives as reflections of ourselves. They help us to realize that what we think about and whom we surround ourselves with greatly influences our energy field and our intrinsic energetic power. So, try to become less reactive to energy vampires' actions—be proactive. Keep your own energy in alignment by *responding* to energy vampires instead of *reacting* to them. In other words, when you spot an energy vampire, instead of feeling that they are robbing you of energy, see the gift they are offering you. They are asking you—consciously or unconsciously—to listen to your emotions, and to tap into the parts of you that need healing.

When you tap into your own soul, you can release energetic blocks caused by past trauma, pain, or loss. Once you have learned the lessons that are the inherent gifts in these blockages—and thereby become more in tune with your soul—you'll become empowered and energy vampires will no longer be able to draw on your energy.

However, there is a note of caution here. As you go through this purification process, as you allow more of your soul's light to enter your physical body, be aware that you can begin to attract many "moths to your flame." Your efforts to align your energetic field can be very attractive to lower vibrational beings. When you are shining brightly, you can cast light upon the shadows within others and can cause their shadow-selves to surface. They can become irritated and moody just by your presence—this is because the light you project is calling their shadows forth. So, while you may no longer be giving your energy away to energy vampires, you may still be attracting energy freeloaders who seek to bask in your light.

Many empaths, light workers, and sensitives are subject to this kind of energy exchange. They can be extremely sensitive to others' feelings and can even start to absorb them as their own. So, caution is the watchword—if you feel depleted energetically, do not succumb to energy-freeloaders, and do not blame your energy depletion on others. Instead, become aware that regulating your energy output is entirely *your responsibility*. After all, we are here to master energy—not to let energy master us!

By pulling ourselves back into alignment and observing ourselves from a spiritual perceptive (being a fly on the wall, so to speak), we can gain conscious awareness of our thoughts and emotions. We can become an observer, instead of blaming others for our emotional health and well-being. As we do this more and more, we will strengthen our energy bodies and learn to regulate our energy productively.

As we strengthen our energetic bodies, it becomes easier—even second nature—to remain in a state of allowing, whereby pure source energy can flow through us. This is not easy, but just as we must go to the gym to burn off extra calories and to strengthen our physical bodies; we must exercise our energetic bodies. Similarly, we need to strengthen our mental, emotional, and spiritual bodies for our spiritual health. Again, this can be difficult, but with practice it becomes easier to avoid getting pulled into others' dramas.

Learning to tune into how others' energies make us feel assists us in becoming stronger. We must develop our energy shield so we do not attract vampires, freeloaders, and parasites. We can be with these types of people without losing our self-awareness. Through the practice of energy mindfulness, we can tap into our own abundant, free-flowing power and maintain our personal alignment.

When we consciously begin to master our own energy awareness, we simultaneously evolve our souls. But as we do this work, as we live our daily lives, and as we attain a more heightened state of consciousness, we will continue to be tested. Just remember that when we feel uncomfortable, pressured, or challenged, this is a sign that an opportunity for growth is available to us. When we take time, when we open our hearts and minds, and when we set the intention to transcend any vibration that does not serve us, growth and expansion results. We will have many ups and downs, yet we can always pull ourselves back into alignment if we are ever-mindful of the energy we are receiving and projecting. Remember—as we have already noted, it takes the same amount of energy to make ourselves happy and strong as it does to make ourselves miserable and weak. The Law of Attraction only responds to what we are offering as a vibration.

So, are you ready to get started? Below are some simple questions to ask yourself and some easy steps to help you tune into your energy body and attain energetic mastery. You'll need your journal and some quiet time to get the most benefit out of doing this exercise. Go ahead—it's time to jump into partnership with your energy field!

Are You Ready to Flow?

1. What is my energy field telling me, right now? For example, is my energy challenging me to be compassionate, to extend forgiveness, to practice self-love, and to practice non-judgement? Write down everything that comes to mind, be easy with yourself.
2. Am I being tested to transcend a difficult situation or conversation right now? How can I do this without reacting from a place of ego? Make a list of all of the ways your ego

tries to pull you out of alignment with the higher-vibration energy of love and acceptance.
3. Am I energetically fragmented right now? What signs can I recognize that my energy is not flowing? For example, am I experiencing mood swings; confusion; chest pains; or sadness for no reason? Am I feeling unbalanced or ungrounded? Am I experiencing physical, mental, or emotional exhaustion? Let your thoughts and emotions flow freely and get it all down on paper. Then, let it all go. You'll feel freer, lighter, and energized.

When we become energetically exhausted, that's a sign that it's time to take care of our emotional and energetic states. Don't judge these moments as "good" or "bad," just recognize them as little reminders to pay attention to your thoughts and feelings. No one can do this for you, it's your responsibility to take care, take action, and regain your power!

Ten Easy Ways to Empower Yourself:

1. Meditate – Engaging in a daily meditation practice is the fastest way to pull more cosmic energy into your body and to gain clarity in any situation.
2. Become conscious – Being mindful of what you are thinking about throughout the day is a really powerful practice. Remember, *what you focus on grows*. Carry a journal with you and write your thoughts down—after a while you'll find yourself taking control of your thoughts. Instead of being influenced by your thoughts, you will be motivated by what you *choose* to think—on purpose!
3. Smudge – Using sacred sage, doing a smudging ceremony can assist you in releasing energetic cords or amplified emotional blocks that may be hindering your forward progress.

4. Call on Your Angels – Ask your angels, out loud, to assist you in removing any energetic blocks that prevent source energy from flowing freely, right now. Remember, angels can only intervene when they are asked to do so, so speak your request out loud, and be specific!
5. Walk in Nature – As often as you can, step away from your environment and culture and take a walk in nature. Get quiet and let the earth and the cosmos balance you on all levels—physically, emotionally, mentally, and spiritually.
6. Take Alone Time – When you step away from situations and people that are evoking confusion or stirring up negative feelings for you, you can easily find clarity about what is actually going on.
7. Be grateful – When you focus on gratitude, your vibration is lifted.
8. Forgive – When you extend forgiveness to others for the harm they have caused you, you clear energetic blockages of unresolved emotions and free yourself. Remember, *forgiveness is for you*.
9. Protect Yourself – Claim your energetic space! When you are out in the world, put an energetic shield around yourself by imagining that you are surrounded by a blue translucent bubble of light. As you create this light shield, confidently declare that only positive, loving energy can enter your personal space.
10. Be accountable – When you take full responsibility for your own energy management, when you create boundaries between yourself and others, and when you decide to love yourself *first*, you empower yourself and your life begins to change—for the better, forever.

5

Intuition - Our Soul's Navigation

"Those who seek outside of themselves become lost, those who seek within remember they're already home."
—Chantelle Renee

The process of remembering and reconnecting to our own Divinity and to All That Is And Ever Has Been is the most profound and fulfilling journey we can take. When opening our awareness to spiritual thoughts and teachings, it is wise to take only what resonates within our hearts and to leave the rest. Spiritual teachings are best suited as guides or catalysts for our own exploration and for connecting to the source within.

So, try not to adopt others' beliefs as your own. Remember: what you are seeking is already within you.

Exercise

By staying in constant dialogue with your soul, you will begin to uncover an inner voice that knows the answers to the questions you are asking. The more you explore, the more answers you will receive. Being constantly present will assist you in *knowing* that *you* are the creator, *you* are the healer, *you* are the guru. Being authentic and transparent with and for yourself will set you free from many self-limiting behaviors.

Practice the exercise below during your day-to-day conversations and activities. Be fully present within your body and your mind. Observe how you feel, what you see, and what you hear. If you feel blockages or resistance, focus on the ideal solution to the block or resistance.

Then, formulate a question or series of questions that will help you to overcome the obstacles you are facing and help you to realize your highest intentions in life. Then, ask yourself those questions. For example, you might ask, "Why do I feel this way? Why do I react this way? Why do I stay this way?" This is how you get to know yourself without the input of others, and without acting upon the projections of others who think they know you.

As you begin to get the answers you are seeking, focus on the solution to the problem you are experiencing right now. If you find that you are not where you want to be, or that you are not living to your fullest potential, have a *real conversation* with yourself. It may feel a little weird at first—but keep doing it.

For example...

Once you have formulated your question(s), and posed the question(s) to yourself, ask yourself: "How do I feel in my body?" Notice that with every bit of negative self-talk or doubt, there is an opposing, empowering thought. For example, you might ask, "What do I want to do in my life?" and get the answer, "I have no idea what I'm here to do, I'm not capable of finding my truth." Opposing thoughts in this situation might be: "I know what I am doing, I am capable of creating."

Try this exercise and see how it works for you. Such self-talk conversations offer you insight into how and why you are "keeping yourself small" and help to strengthen your intuition. You have everything you need—it resides inside of you. Trust yourself! Believe in yourself!

The act of intentionally reaching and purposefully seeking to connect with the Divine pulls us forward on the path to our highest alignment. The Divine will always show us the way; it is our choice as to how we choose to receive and perceive its messages. The Divine always invites us to return home, our job is to *allow*, and to embrace our power as an eternal child of light. As we begin to ignite our sacred light, we gain profound insight and intuitive sensibilities, and we come to realize that transformation is not only our highest path, it is our birthright.

Intuition is one of the greatest gifts we are given to help us on the path of transformation. This gift, our so-called *sixth sense*, enables us to perceive things beyond the physical realm. Everyone possesses psychic abilities, though most of us go through life not realizing the vast potential that lies within us. If you can trust your intuitive gift, it can lead to amazing changes in your life.

Many of us are not sure how to hear or receive clear communication from the nether realms and our minds and egos can twist or diminish the wisdom that comes to us through our intuition. Our minds and egos like to keep us limited to what *we think we know*. We can feel confused as to what direction to take in life, we can feel pushed and pulled—by our loved ones, even by the society we live in. This can leave us in a state of confusion and chaos, so it is important to take time to silence the mind and the ego, in order to hear our inner guidance system—our soul's intuition.

Remember, it is not the mind or the ego, but rather the *heart* that the soul calls to lead the way. As we move into our heart, into our feelings, we find our connection to All That Is. You will always know whether or not what you pick up intuitively is the truth by the way it makes you *feel* in your heart—your heart always tells you the truth.

As noted earlier, the heart is an intelligent, electromagnetic powerhouse. When the heart is free-flowing, we can hear, see, and feel its clear signals, and we can receive its guidance via our intuition. For example, I feel at home in my heart. I find that when I go into my heart center, it is easy to invoke emotions that can then connect me to my intuition. As I go into my heart, I feel powerful and aligned. In this space, I can sense my angels, guides, and the supreme presence of All That Is.

By tuning into your feelings, you too can begin to connect with your higher self, your angels, and your guides—and then follow the guidance they offer. Learning to trust your intuition is the key to strengthening your channel into the unified field around you—and the key to trusting your intuition is listening to your heart.

The unseen, unified field that encompasses everything around us and within us also *informs us*. We must learn to flow with and sense this subtle energy, we must not try to control it, we must simply *allow it*. To awaken this dormant potential in ourselves, we must heal the wounds that weaken our connection—self-doubt, unworthiness, shame—all these limiting beliefs can make us feel less than the amazing beings we are! It's time to banish those beliefs and tap into our intuitive, Divine wisdom!

Trusting in our intuition is truly how we align with the Divine. As we tune into our true essence as eternal, spiritual beings, as we trust our spirit's guidance, we flow, we create, we allow, and we are present and at peace. Our intuition reaches beyond the limited space and time that we know in our everyday experience. When we explore the depths of being one with All That Is, when we open our hearts, free our minds, and trust fully in the Divine, we find that we are supported and loved.

Learning to attune to the guidance of the Divine is empowering—and your intuition is the best tool to use to navigate life's challenges and to help you steer your life in the direction you want to go. Your intuition can lead you to your passion—a passion you may have never known you had. If you don't believe this, think back to a time when a still, small voice inside you told you not to do something and you didn't listen. Later, you said, "I knew I shouldn't have done that!" That voice was your intuition—it has always been with you, and it always has your best interests at heart. But, too often the voice of the intuition is so very quiet—it is hard to hear. But, knowing that, it's easy to begin tapping in, and listening on a deeper level.

Here is a tried-and-true exercise to help you tap into your intuition. As you begin, it is important to not be rigid or to hold high expectations—this can create energetic resistance. Just go slow, have fun, and look at this exercise as an adventure. Learning to tap into your intuition is much like unlocking a treasure chest of Divine gifts. Tapping in will not only bring more meaning and clarity to your life but also will give you a heightened sense of power within.

Ready?

Feel into your Heart Space

> *When you are trying to make a decision, pose a question to yourself that reflects the circumstances you are in as a "Yes" or "No" answer. Then, get quiet, breathe, feel into your heart space, and feel your response to the question. Do you feel a great resistance? That's a "No" answer. Or, do you feel your energy expanding? That's a "Yes" answer!*

As noted, intuition is about *feeling* and *being*, rather than physically *seeing* with your eyes. We all receive intuitive guidance in various unique ways, depending upon our own methods of receptivity. In psychic and mediumship jargon, these methods are called "the Clairs." Each of these Clairs can be broken down into sub-categories, but for now, see if you can tune into the Clairs you feel the most connected to. From there, you can begin to open yourself up more to receiving Divine guidance by honing in on just one of the Clairs, and practicing to strengthen that particular ability. As you begin to practice your own psychic awareness, as you begin to listen without resisting or judging, your intuition will be strengthened. Soon, your intuitive processes will begin to flow effortlessly.

Your Clair Senses

The word Clair means "Clear" and "The Clairs" include any and all types of psychic sensitivity that correspond to the senses. They are named to specify the way we sense and receive information spiritually.

- Seeing (Clairvoyance),
- Hearing (Clairaudience),

- Feeling (Clairsentience),
- Smelling (Clairscent),
- Tasting (Clairgustance),
- Touching (Clairtangency),
- Empathizing (Clairempathy),
- Knowing (Claircognizance).

Clairvoyance

Clairvoyance (clear vision) – To reach into another vibrational frequency and to visually perceive "within the mind's eye" something existing in that other realm. A Clairvoyant receives extrasensory impressions and symbols in the form of "inner sight," or mental images which are perceived without the aid of the physical eyes, beyond the limitations of ordinary time and space. These impressions are more easily perceived in an Alpha state and during meditation, though many Clairvoyants can obtain visual information regarding the past, present, and future in a variety of environments.

Clairaudience

Clairaudience (clear hearing) – To perceive sounds, words, or extrasensory noise from sources broadcast from spiritual or ethereal realms, in the form of "inner ear" receptivity or mental tones which are perceived without the aid of the physical ear and beyond the limitations of ordinary time and space. These tones and vibrations are more easily perceived in an Alpha state and during meditation, though many Clairaudients can obtain verbal and sound-related information regarding the past, present, and future in a variety of environments. Most channelers (also known as Mediums, see below) work with both Clairvoyance and Clairaudience.

Clairsentience

Clairsentience (clear sensation or feeling) – To perceive information via a "feeling" within the whole body, without any outer stimuli related to the feeling or information (see also Clairempathy).

Clairscent

Clairscent (clear smelling) – To smell a fragrance/odor (e.g. a substance or a food) which is not in one's surroundings. These odors are perceived without the aid of the physical nose and beyond the limitations of ordinary time and space.

Clairtangency

Clairtangency (clear touching) – More commonly known as "psychometry." To handle an object or touch an area and perceive through the palms of one's hands information about the article or its owner or history that was not previously known by the clairtangent.

Clairgustance

Clairgustance (clear tasting) – To taste a substance without putting anything in one's mouth. It is claimed that those who possess this ability are able to perceive the essence of a substance from the spiritual or ethereal realms through taste.

Clairempathy

Clairempathy (clear emotion) – An empath is a person who can psychically tune in to the emotional experience of a person, place, or animal. Clairempathy is a type of telepathy in which one can sense or feel, within one's self, the attitude, emotion, or ailment of another person or entity. Empaths tune into the vibrations and "feel" the tones of the aura.

Claircognizance

Claircognizance is sometimes called the super-power clair, because it does not engage any of the physical senses—and yet it engages them all. A claircognizant individual receives psychic information that is accurate but they have no human-sense reference to say "how" they know what they know, they "just know." This clair is the most difficult to clarify, because what the knower knows is *intrinsic*, it is not known in the mind nor is it known in any individual sense, it just "is."

Channel/Channeling

A channel is a medium who allows his/her body and mind to be used as a mechanism for etheric world intelligence to bring psychic information or healing energy to others. I do not recommend opening yourself up to other beings, unless you are shown proper ways to keep yourself safe. Always work in the spirit of love and light, and seek someone who is a specialist in this area to help you before trying to channel on your own.

The act of channeling involves a channeler allowing an etheric world intelligence to enter their mind and impress thoughts upon their consciousness. The channeler uses their own voice or body to deliver the information or healing energy.

Different channelers engage with different entities—sometimes the energies they bring through from the higher planes and netherworlds are the departed spirits of those who previously lived human lives. Sometimes the energies are higher-vibrational beings from other worlds who come to bring the sitter (the person consulting the medium or channeler) messages that can help direct them in their lives. And sometimes, the channeler is bringing through communications from 'a spirit guide' or an angelic presence.

We all have angels and guides—and they communicate by sending us messages. These can come through in various ways: seeing physical signs and symbols, hearing music on the radio, seeing images on television, hearing high-pitched ringing in your ears, seeing numbers, even hearing words from external sources or within your mind. For example, you might repeatedly find dimes or feathers in unexpected locations, and if there is simply no explanation for how they got there, these may be communications from your angels. You might see numbers repeated in various locations (e.g. seeing the numbers 11:11 on your clock, on addresses, in magazines, on billboards, etc.). Be open to receive and embrace these messages as they appear, for they are intended to comfort and lovingly guide you. Pay attention to the subtle signs around you, but remember, not every sign is going to appear on a big billboard on the side of the road!

Similarly, synchronicities experienced in everyday life can indicate that gifts are flowing to you from the universe—synchronicities are often confirmations from our angels that we are aligned with our intentions. When synchronistic events occur in your life, say "thank you" and bless your angels for the love they offer. They appreciate receiving your gratitude.

By being grateful and feeling humble for the guidance and love angels and guides offer, we create a clear communication channel so we can engage in clear and open communication with them. Thanking them and extending an invitation to them to walk with you is a great way to fine-tune your relationship with them. Remember, if you want help from your angels, you must ask for it—for due to the principle of free will they cannot interfere in your affairs without your permission (although they will intervene if an accident is about to befall you that would result in your death—if the timing does not reflect your "blueprint" for this lifetime). You can develop your own personal appeal to call your angels to you. An invitation such as this one can help to bring them to you in an instant: *"I call upon my angels and guides to walk by my side, please offer me guidance, discipline, council, help, and love. Thank you."*

Working with Your Guides

We all have spirit guides that are with us to assist in our daily life choices and experiences. They are always around us—just a thought away, whether we are aware of their presence or not. Learning to connect with them consciously can be a powerful and effective way to develop your intuitive abilities. The more you work with your guides, the clearer and more effortless the connection will be. There are many different ways of opening up to trust and allow guidance from your angels to come through. These include such practices as saying affirmations, meditating, sitting in silence, dream journaling, using metaphysical tools, etc. Above all, take care of your body and your heart-space, for your diet, level of exercise, and overall physical and emotional conditions can affect your psychic abilities greatly. Our intuition flows through our physical, mental, spiritual, and emotional bodies, so taking care of *all of you* is the key to accessing your intuition with the most clarity.

As you hone your psychic ability, practice staying open to receiving knowledge and guidance far beyond anything you can conceptualize. The universe may surprise you with all manner of signs, symbols, and experiences that you have not encountered in the past. Remember, the mind wants to make everything logical and practical, but the spirit is *magical*. We can never understand the vastness or complexity of the Divine Design, so be ready to receive, and trust that the universe intends only the best for you.

As you work with some of the methods noted below, remember to ask your angels for guidance. Your angels and guides dwell outside of space and time, and, as noted, if called upon, they will be by your side instantly. We don't have to do everything alone, however, we cannot expect an answer from our angels until we are ready and willing to receive it, and until we can trust that our angels are indeed always there for us when we need them. Trusting the information you receive is a key factor in becoming an accurate intuitive. The more you practice trusting your intuitive process, the better you will become! Methods to use to connect with your helpers and guides include:

- Affirmations – psychic ability increases when you take chances with your perceptions, accepting them, stating them boldly, out loud. You can do this by using affirmations on a daily basis until you feel that you have accepted subconsciously that you do indeed have psychic abilities and are capable of employing them successfully. Here are a few affirmations that can help you tap in:

    - *My clairs, telepathy, intuition, and all my psychic abilities increase every day.*
    - *The higher power of the universe is guiding me through my intuitive senses.*
    - *I am open to receive the wisdom and intelligence of Source.*
    - *My inner vision is always focused and clear.*
    - *I am worthy of accessing my gifts.*
    - *I radiate joy and love.*

- Meditation – A sure method of improving your psychic ability is to practice regular meditation. Psychic ability, at its core, is attuning to the spirit. To increase your psychic contact with the universe, it is important to train yourself to reach your center effortlessly. There are many different methods of meditation and you will likely find a meditation class at your local community center. After just a few lessons, you will be able to meditate effectively on your own.

- Dream Journaling – Your dreams can offer important insights for your spiritual journey. Keep a dream journal and your favorite pen on your nightstand, and write down your dreams as soon as you awaken each day.

- Angel Cards – Using angel cards can assist you in strengthening your connection to the angelic realm and in being confident about the guidance your angels offer. Angel cards support your spiritual and earthly journey and guide you past the most common challenges in our physical world—transcending fear and embracing love. When working with angel cards, be sure to surround yourself with a bubble of white light filled with love and serenity—and invite the angels in.

- Metaphysical Tools – There are number of metaphysical tools you can use to help you develop and improve your psychic abilities. Tarot cards, for example, can help you to interpret messages from the nether world and divining rods and pendulums can be used for measuring energy fields and answering questions. All of these tools are easy to learn to use.

Remember, when you use any metaphysical tool or engage in any spiritual practice, you are in dialogue with your higher self and your spirit guides. You may sometimes feel that you are lost in unknown territory—again, your local community center or spiritual bookstore will have classes and mentors to help you with these tools and techniques.

As you practice connecting with your angels and guides, remember to set your intention to connect only with loving, benevolent spirits. And, when you tap into the higher vibrational realms, if you want to be sure you are truly connected with your angels and spirit guides, check in with your emotions. Discernment is one of the gifts of the Holy Spirit and it is extremely important to cultivate it when you are doing this work. So, ask yourself, "How do I feel?" If you feel safe, loved, and guided, then you are attuned to the gentle and subtle presence of a master, a spirit guide, or an angel. If you feel scared, nervous, fearful, or judged, then you are not attuned to a higher energetic being. Love is the emotion that dominates life in the higher realms. A lower vibrational being will stir up lower vibrational emotions of fear, greed, revenge, or hate. If you ever find yourself experience these kinds of emotions when you are connecting with the spirit world, do not worry. Simply imagine yourself surrounded by the white, loving light of the Holy Spirit and send out vibrations of unconditional love. The higher vibration of love will always banish lower energetic frequencies. Love, generated outward from your heart space, will keep you safe.

Whenever you are following your intuitive 'hits' (the messages you receive), let your heart be your guide. Remember, Spirit has your back, you came here to experience and thrive. You must open your mind and your heart far beyond this physical world to receive your highest good from All That Is Divine. Remember, all that you need is coming to you, and all that you want is unfolding in perfect time. So, let your angels and your spirit helpers guide you. Remember—the kingdom of heaven resides *inside* of you. You alone are the keeper of the wisdom you have been searching for. You're no less than the stars in the sky—you are destined to shine!

6

Breaking the Chains - Limiting Core Beliefs

"Our consciousness expands into new dimensions as we explore outside others' preconceived notions."
—Chantelle Renee

What is a belief? A belief is a powerful, dense, emotion-based thought with immense power to direct our lives and affect our inner monologue—that inner conversation we all have with ourselves about how we perceive the world around us. But where do our beliefs come from? By and large, in our modern societies, we borrow them. Too often, we adopt others' beliefs as our own without questioning them. As children, for example, we are brought up with standards and belief systems that our families, our societies, and our religions have set in place for us—we have not been encouraged to think for ourselves. We have been influenced greatly by those who are most important to us in our lives. Our parents and our peers have shaped—and still shape—the way we see ourselves and the world around us.

When we adopt others' beliefs as our own, these often-limiting beliefs can keep us from growing and expanding to our greatest potential. This can be especially true when we have never questioned anything others have told us, and have simply accepted their word as fact. When we do this, in essence, a state of spiritual paralysis takes place within us—by not holding a personal belief system that resonates with our soul's purpose, we inhibit our own soul's growth.

A belief is your thought of what your truth is and, like it or not, your beliefs both reflect and create your current reality. So, challenging the beliefs of others that you hold as your own is key to living your life fully, shedding the veils that keeping you separate from *God*/Source, reaching your fullest potential as a human being and as a soul, and becoming one with All That Is.

Since every experience in our lives is fueled by our belief systems, it is important to reevaluate our belief systems often so as to not become complacent or be led astray. Ultimately, we don't want to live our lives on 'auto pilot,' controlled by others. Instead, we want to drive our own (soul) vehicle consciously.

Sometimes, however, our thoughts can block us from moving in the direction we want to go and our minds play tricks on us, causing us to doubt that our basic needs will be met. Consequently, we spend much of our time in 'survival' mode, ignoring our dreams and our life goals and moving instead at cross purposes to our true intentions. Once we identify what our actual needs are, however, and once we examine how our belief systems are affecting our reality, we can see how we create resistance through the beliefs we hold, how we operate from fear, and how we place ourselves into a "lack mentality."

Fear is a heavy, dense emotion that can distress us, and in order to conquer it, we must look first at what fundamental belief has precipitated the fear. We must ask ourselves, "What belief do I need to shift in order to get what I want?" For example, if you want to be loved but you believe that you are unworthy of love, you need to shift your belief from *fearing* that you will never be loved to *knowing* that you are worthy of love.

Beliefs can act either as anchors on our consciousness or as catalysts, launching us forward into new perspectives and new experiences. If your current beliefs hinder you, you may want to explore new beliefs that support your spiritual growth. For example, if you are judgmental of others, or you have expectations of others, you may be setting yourself up for suffering or disappointment. You are the only one who can make these shifts as they are internal and unique to your experience. If your beliefs are not yours but have instead been borrowed from others, remember, your consciousness can only begin to expand if you explore beyond the preconceived notions that you have adopted from others. Try to not cling to anyone else's truth—your truth awaits your discovery. Try each day to fuel your curiosity and to birth a personal belief system that reflects your soul's purpose and that resonates deeply with you. When you shift your own belief systems, you manifest new experiences.

When you begin to explore your belief systems and release the beliefs that do not resonate with you, you may be surprised to discover how much freer you feel. In order to get to the core of your beliefs and stop them from controlling you, become an observer, shine the light of awareness on the beliefs you hold unconsciously. Observe, for example, how other people have projected their beliefs about themselves, their religion, their lifestyle, etc. upon you and how you have accepted them as your own.

When one of your beliefs triggers you emotionally, follow the feeling to its core. When you become angry, for example, ask yourself, "Why am I feeling this emotion? Where does it stem from?

Is it based in a childhood experience I had personally—or is it based in something an adult told me when I was a child? Is it an emotion I still want to have when similar situations arise?"

Because your thoughts are anchored into your limited belief systems, your thoughts drive your emotions, and your emotions communicate your intentions into the energy field around you, your beliefs determine your reality. But, when you become an observer observing, you can identify which of the core beliefs you hold work against you—and then you can take action to change them.

Be Present with Yourself

As we explore our resistance, we become aware of our ignorance.

By staying in constant dialogue with your soul, you will begin to discover your inner voice. You already know the answers you are seeking! The more questions you explore, the more answers you will receive.

Being consistently present with yourself will help you to get in touch with your inner knowing. You are the creator, the healer, and the guru—being authentic and transparent with yourself will set you free from self-limiting behaviors.

Exercise

During your day-to-day conservations and activities, be fully present in your body and mind. Observe how you feel, what you see, what you hear.

Ask questions that serve your highest intentions in life. This is how you get to "know thyself," without others projecting upon you who they think you are or who they want you to be.

As you begin to get the answers you are seeking, focus on the solutions. If you are not where you want to be, if you are not living your fullest potential, have a real conversation with yourself. It may feel a little weird at first. Keep doing it.

For example, ask:

- *Why do I feel this way?*
- *Why do I react this way?*
- *Why do I stay this way?*

Focus on resolving the block or resistance. How do you feel in your body? Remember, with every negative 'self-talk thought' of doubt there is an opposing, empowering thought.

| An answer you may get: | *I am not worthy of that job, I am not smart enough.* |
| An opposition would be: | *I am worthy of that job and I love to learn as I go.* |

These conversations will offer you insight into how you are keeping yourself small and will help strengthen your intuition.

Core Beliefs

What is a core belief? Core beliefs are the thoughts a person has that determine how they interpret their experiences. For example, if someone has the core belief that "the world is a bad place," they will believe that people who are kind have ulterior motives (because someone being kind without a discernible reason just doesn't line up with their worldview). Challenging such negative core beliefs can help you to develop a healthier understanding of yourself and the world around you.

As another example, say you don't like meeting new people. Your core belief could be that you are insecure and fear rejection, so you have subconsciously built walls around yourself because you believe others will not embrace you or you believe others have nothing to offer you.

As you begin to illuminate your beliefs, you can make a list of how that belief serves you, hinders you, or limits your forward progress. Once you become an observer, you can begin to unravel the limitations and choose consciously what you want your new beliefs to be. You want to disempower limited beliefs by replacing them with new beliefs, based on evidence that you yourself discover. Look at things, for example, from your personal perspective, not from the perspective assigned by the belief you hold. Question things from a place of non-judgement. As you affirm that you can break down old beliefs and replace them with beliefs that resonate with you, the universe supports you.

Remember, when you reprogram your beliefs, you reclaim your power. Your brain is like a computer and your mind is programmable. If you are not the one who is programming it, somebody else will. Your energy flows where your attention goes and when you align your belief systems, your thoughts and emotions match the frequency of that desire. As you step into your power as a conscious creator, magic happens!

This is why we must take responsibility for our own beliefs as the manifesters of our own lives. Right here, right now, we have the power to break the chains that bind us. As we begin to illuminate our core beliefs, as we make our unconscious belief systems conscious, we step out of a limited way of viewing ourselves and the world and we shift into a whole new perspective.

Subtle shifts in perception bring forth big shifts in healing. As we expand and look through different lenses of potential, we free ourselves from the enslavement of our limiting beliefs. With our newfound awareness, we step into our unlimited selves, into a realm brimming with infinite possibilities for manifestation.

Shifting Your Core Beliefs Worksheet

The simple exercises below can help you to see that while you have lots of emotionally charged thoughts, they are not all *subjective truths*. Recognizing the difference between fact and opinion can assist you in challenging the dysfunctional or harmful opinions you have about yourself and others. Remain open to allowing new truths to unfold and new perspectives to surface as you shift your beliefs!

Take some time to journal and answer the questions below in detail. Make a list (honestly and transparently) of how each of your beliefs serves or hinders you. The ultimate questions to ask when challenging your beliefs are:

- What is your belief about creation and its origin?
- What is your belief about the concepts of *good* and *bad*?
- What is your belief about *unconditional love*?
- What are your society's expectations / beliefs about lifestyle, religion, and career?
- What are the values of someone close you?
    - What are your father's core values?
    - What are your mother's core values?
- What is your belief about your self-worth? For example:
    - I am too fat.
    - I am not smart enough.
    - I am not loveable.
    - I will never have enough money.
    - Do you believe you are worthy?
    - Do you believe you must go to college to be successful?
    - Do you feel that your reality is fixed and there is no way to change it?
    - Add your own self-worth questions here.

Now, for each of these beliefs, ask yourself these questions:

- Does this belief reflect the truth of who I am?
- How does this belief affect me, positively or negatively?
- How does this belief affect my life decisions?
- How does this belief make feel?
- Is this belief a borrowed projection?
- Is this belief the absolute truth for me?

Do you want to change your beliefs? Remember, if you are not the one programming your belief systems, somebody else will. So, ask yourself these questions:

- What do I think a belief is?
- What experience led me to have each of my beliefs?
- What holds me back from breaking the chains that bind me to my beliefs?

Then ask yourself these questions about each of the beliefs on the first bullet list above:

- Where did I get this belief?
- Why am I emotionally tied to this belief?
- Why do I choose to make this my "belief to live by?"
- Why is this belief good or bad?
- What is the emotional pay-off for me in keeping this belief, if it hinders my expansion?
- What is the pay-off generally in my life for keeping this hindering belief?
- What is my resistance to letting this belief go?

Now, if you feel prepared to change your beliefs, ask yourself these questions:

- Who am I?
- Where did my first sense of individuality come from?
- What values do I want to live by?
- What new beliefs can I claim as mine that feel best for my journey?
- What other options are there that would benefit me?

When you choose to reprogram and shed your limiting beliefs, your commitment to change can be met with resistance—by your family and friends, even by your own mind. Old habits can be challenging to break! Financial pressure and popular media beliefs can also influence your resolve to change. But, resistance can be used as a catalyst—so every time you notice any resistance rising, remember your commitment to change and reclaim your sacred energies.

Conversely, resistance can cause you to sink before you swim. If you wish to raise your vibrational frequency and align with the Divine, you must diligently practice the conscious awareness of your thoughts and emotions, and focus on the thoughts you want to bring into manifestation. Remember: *what you think, you create.* What you bring into conscious awareness becomes reality. If you allow old, outdated beliefs that others instilled in you to be the driving forces in your life, they will be. So, burrow down into your subconscious mind and examine your core beliefs, then shed the beliefs you no longer wish to have. This is the way to transform your core beliefs.

Our lives only change when we make what is *unconscious* conscious. Ideally, we want to move from a limited, contracted state of being into an expansive, flexible state of being. As you become more aware of what your core beliefs have been, and as you continuously cast off beliefs that hinder your forward progress, you will become more in tune with the world around you. You will begin to notice others' beliefs and how they influence you, and you can discern whether they resonate with the 'new you.' If they do, you can adopt them as your own. You and you alone can choose consciously what you will accept and what you will not accept.

The exercise below is designed to assist you in illuminating your unconsciously-held (or 'borrowed') beliefs and to challenge them by observing and questioning them. This will take some deep reflection as you have nourished your beliefs for years—through negative thinking, self-doubt, and worry. Often, our limiting beliefs are to blame for the lack of change in our lives. Our dreams can come true, if we just get out of our own way!

To release limiting beliefs, we must simply address the root of the belief itself. We must get to the deeper feelings attached to each belief and discover where it came from. This can be a simple—and empowering—process, if you are open to it.

Ready to be inspired? Get out your journal and your favorite pen, and find a quiet space where you can be alone for a while. As you go through each question below, take notice of your first thought and the emotional reaction that follows it—write down that answer. Don't over-think it!

Journaling

What is the limited belief you hold that most interferes with you living your best life?

We all have limiting beliefs that we have picked up from past experiences and from other people. What is the most predominate belief that keeps you from growing and moving in the direction of your joy or passion? That you're not smart? That you're not worthy? That you aren't 'good enough'? That you don't have enough money?

That you aren't lovable? Write that belief (or those beliefs) down and then go through the four questions below.

The Ultimate Questions to Ask When Challenging a Belief:

Use these questions when you find a belief you want to challenge.

1. Where did this limiting belief come from? Is it someone else's or is it my own? (If it is borrowed, where or from whom did this belief come? [e.g. personal experiences, people you know, society, religion, the government]).

   Write down every answer that comes to your mind.

2. Does this belief serve me or hinder me? Does it support me in following my dreams and living an empowered life? Does it affect me positive or negatively?

   Write down all the reasons that the belief does or does not support or affect you.

3. Is this belief an *absolute truth*? Can this belief be seen from a different perspective or is it solid and unchangeable? What proof do I have that this belief is a fact?

   Write down all the reasons that this belief is not a fact.

4. How can I shift this belief to make it work for me? (Create new beliefs that support and serve you in your spiritual growth. Don't play small! Remember, you are stepping out

of fear and limitation into faith and abundance.) How does your new belief feel?

Example:
Old belief: I can't become a business owner. It is too risky and I don't have the money to start it. Things don't really work out for me in business.
New belief: I can have my own business and I will put out the focus, drive, and energy to manifest it. The universe is on my side.

Use the science of the spoken word to anchor your new belief. Try speaking positive affirmations that support your new belief systems several times each day. For example:

I am capable of anything I put my heart, mind, and soul into. I am worthy of abundance in all areas of my life. I am supported by the universe.

When you speak this affirmation, do you feel it in your body, your heart, and your soul? Remember, *you have to believe it to receive it!*

7

Relationships: Mirrors for our Expansion

> "I am a reflection of you and you are a reflection of me, it is within our heart's transparency that we will begin to truly see."
> —Chantelle Renee

The relationships in our lives are our greatest gifts and our greatest teachers. They offer us companionship, shared experiences, they teach us to trust and to love, they provide us with family and opportunities to co-create, they promote growth, and so on. Relationships challenge us, they lift us up and lower us. Those we are in relationship with love us and they hate us—and everything in-between.

We could not expand our souls without having relationships. We came here not only to experience true love but also to experience messy love, painful love, and lack of love—all of these are lessons on our path back to the unconditional love we descended from.

Many people struggle with relationships. It can be difficult to find balance in interactions with others, to learn to trust those we are in relationship with, and it can be challenging to create a safe haven within relationships in which to flourish and grow without resistance. As you navigate the relationships in your life, it is important to remember that you are not here to change anyone, you are here to evolve *personally*. All relationships are sacred gifts, and learning to nurture them and grow in them will bring peace and understanding to your life. Be grateful, therefore, for both the perceived "bad" and "good" relationships you have experienced—they have all served you on your journey of self-discovery and self-love. All of your relationships serve to reflect your expansion and contraction as an individual. Without them, there could be no contrast, exploration, or growth. As you mature spiritually through your relationships, you are able to explore new levels of interaction with others, and to gain a new appreciation of what it means to be human. In this way, you can experience deep, unconditional, and awakened love.

As you engage in your daily relationships, be mindful that they are mirrors for you—and that just as you are experiencing "the other," and projecting upon them, they too are experiencing you and projecting upon you. As you open your heart and mind to another person in relationship, as you become vulnerable and transparent in your interactions with them, you discover that your true power lies in engaging deeply with one another. If you embrace the idea that "I am a reflection of you and you are a reflection of me," you will deepen your spiritual experience and thereby obtain a deeper intimacy with the other person. You will begin to appreciate that while each individual is unique, everyone is on their own spiritual journey and everyone brings a unique perspective to their relationships. We must, therefore, be open to learning from one another, and we must look at one another as teachers and soul-mates, each of us offering the other an opportunity to learn to love ourselves deeply, so that we in turn can love others freely. Until we are able to do this, we will stay in a cycle of imbalanced relationships. The ultimate achievement is to be able to give and receive love freely, because this is when we are the most aligned with spirit.

We will have many soul-mates on our journeys. Some will inspire us and some will devastate us. Yet, every encounter is a gift that serves us on our path to self-discovery. When we evaluate our past relationships, we can see how they have had a direct impact on our current views. But reflecting on these past experiences is not negative, for our relationships have taught us many priceless lessons and have prepared us for this period in our evolution. To truly learn from our interactions with others, we must observe the past without judgement, we must step out of our egos and into our hearts. Then, we will discover that no matter how our relationships have unfolded, we carry with us the emotional gifts and spiritual lessons that we have acquired from and through them.

Giving and receiving love freely may sound simple; however, it can be difficult. For some people, it's easy to give, but not to receive. For others, it's easy to receive, but not to give. You will never be able give or receive unconditional love and acceptance from another until you can love yourself unconditionally and forgive yourself.

So, the first relationship you need to reflect upon is your relationship with *yourself*. All relationships you may engage in thereafter are reflections of your relationship with yourself. To love yourself is to speak up for what your desires, needs, and wishes are—up front, transparently, with no hidden agenda.

We can only love others the way we love ourselves. As you travel through life and learn the lessons provided in your relationships with others, you discover that you are worthy of love that can meet you in your depths as well as in your shallows. You must learn to love yourself deeply, for we can only meet another in the depths that we have met ourselves in. We can often project upon others how we expect them to love us, but it's important to remember that others can love you only in the way they love themselves. They can only meet you in the depths of love they have been in themselves. Expecting that another's love will fill you up will always fall short. First, you must love yourself, all else will follow.

> "Become less reactivate to others' actions, and become proactive in the awareness of yours. This is the path of self-mastery."
> —Chantelle Renee

Practicing Non-Judgement

> "When we send love in response to hate, we become spiritual alchemists."
> —Wayne Dyer

Imagine if we all agreed to allow others simply to just be, without casting our projections of limitation and judgement upon them! The selfless act of loving everyone unconditionally would dissolve so many conflicts—within ourselves, with others, and with everyone everywhere, around the globe. If only we could all understand that all of us, in all our uniqueness, are expressions of Divinity.

While that is an ideal way of looking at the world, it is prudent to ask ourselves, "Who are we, really, to say who is right or who is wrong? Who are we to judge someone else?" We are all here, in our own realities, expanding, contracting, and experiencing—for ourselves as individuals, for each other, and for the collective consciousness. We are all doing the best we can in relation to what is going on in our personal environments. We all act and react to what occurs in our private worlds according to how we feel or what we think in any given moment. We all act and interact in our own unique ways to things that occur around us, we all perceive what happens to us and around us differently, and we all express ourselves differently.

Because we are all unique, it is safe to say that how we perceive one another's actions and projections is not always accurate to what they intend. We can misunderstand one another easily, unless we stay neutral in our responses and seek clarity where there might otherwise be confusion. We are not all mind-readers and we can take someone else's innocent gesture to whole new (mistaken) heights easily, if we are not careful with our initial judgements.

We all judge people in different ways—sometimes innocently and unintentionally, and sometimes, intentionally and unkindly. We can judge people for trivial reasons—how they spend their money, their speech or mannerisms, their body size, etc., or for more serious reasons—the jobs they have, their sexual preferences, their religious beliefs, the list goes on. It is human nature to judge—our ability to discern the safety of our environment in a milli-second is sometimes crucial to our survival. But controlling our natural impulse to judge when we are safe and secure is another thing entirely. It is important to remember that when we are judging others for social, cultural, or religious reasons—not for reasons of survival—we are in fact judging ourselves.

When we notice that we are judging the actions of others—and hence ourselves—it is helpful to reflect on the fact that we are, by and large, products of our environments. The conditioning our families and society placed upon us (both unintentionally and intentionally) when we were young took our power, before we ever knew how powerful we were. Our early childhood conditioning can keep us in a limited mind space, and we can grow into adulthood with no tools to expand past these limitations or circumstances. As a result, oftentimes, we can stand in judgement of others and we can act out against others, not because we are bad people but because we are lost, misunderstood, and not in alignment with our own souls.

By consciously extending compassion instead of aggression and judgement, we can shift our perspective of ourselves and others in a matter of seconds. Never doubt that you can change someone's life by offering them your unconditional presence and support. We can never know the path another person has walked upon or the pain they have experienced—we can never know what makes another person behave as they do. Remember, people who are hurting can act out in despair, not knowing any other way to express themselves.

Learning not to judge yourself is the gateway to understanding how not to judge others. Judgements can come so easily to us. Judgements often serve as defense mechanisms that we use to compare ourselves to others and to categorize others in order to make ourselves feel better about ourselves. Until you can look at your judgements of yourself and resolve them for good, you will stay in the pattern of judgement—and that can be a vicious cycle. But, if we look at the reasons we judge, we realize that the flaws we perceive in others are the same flaws we see in ourselves. That realization can offer us an opportunity to love ourselves more deeply, to forgive ourselves for our imperfections, and then to allow our love to flow outwards to others more freely.

In a phrase, in order to truly understand our light, we must fully embrace our darkness. And, once we have known the depths of our own darkness, then we can begin to understand the darkness of another. This is a crucial lesson to learn in life, for without this kind of deep self-examination, there can be no expansion. We must come to a place where we realize that in our relationships with others, we must see each individual as part and parcel of who we are. We must be able to look at another person and say, "It is only through the love in our hearts that we begin to truly see what is real—we are all one."

It is the highest of all possible goals to practice this type of "spiritual alchemy" with the souls of the world, sending out unconditional love to all, instead of sending out hate, or disgust, or rage in response to injustice, prejudice, or wrongs. But this ideal can be challenging, especially if you feel that because of someone's behavior, they are undeserving of your love. Sometimes, as well, you may wish to withdraw your love from others because you feel they have withdrawn their love from you. There is the trap! There is the damaging, hopeless cycle that we can get stuck in! To practice sending love instead of hate to everyone who has harmed you, or those you love, or the world—or sending love to those who hate or who hurt others—is healing. Love heals not only you and them, it heals the world. It offers up space for you to love yourself more deeply and unconditionally. By sending love out to all, you are saying, "I love myself deeply and I can love freely." In this way, you elevate yourself as well as them; you master the lesson of forgiveness, and you practice unconditional love.

Thus, whenever someone offends you, or upsets you, or hurts you or someone you love, or you see stories on the news that affront your sensibilities, do not judge. Instead, keep the perpetrators of wrong in your heart and say, "I see you. I love you. I forgive you. I am not here to judge you, I am here to learn from you. I am here to love you." Learning non-judgement and forgiveness is the path to transcendence, it is the path to oneness, and the way to realize your Divinity. There is, after all, no judgement in the presence of All That Is And Ever Has Been.

In the back of this book, there is a *Notes* section. I invite you to take some time to reflect upon how you judge yourself and others. Writing your judgements down can act as a mirror for you and can offer you clarity, helping you to release judgements and to transcend the vicious cycle of judgement. It may help you to remember that we are all at different places of consciousness, that we all came from different backgrounds, that we all have our stories, and that we are all doing the best we can with where we are at, right here, right now. Learning to accept fully where others are at within the vast sea of consciousness will help your soul to evolve spiritually.

> "Love is the absence of judgment."
> —The Dalai Lama

8

Taming the Ego

"The journey into unity consciousness begins as we step out of our egos and into our hearts."
—Chantelle Renee

The ego defines our personalities, allowing us to experience polarity while living in the physical world. The ego (being practical, realistic, and mundane-life-focused as it is) can often try to sabotage our search for spiritual growth and union with the Divine (spirit, being as it is, impractical, ethereal, and transcendence-focused). As human beings, we must learn to mediate between the mandates of our egos and the longings of our souls. We must endeavor to create a harmonious balance between these two disparate aspects within ourselves. To be aware of the ego is to have power over how we choose to give, receive, and express our energy—both our physical energy and our spiritual energy.

Managing the gulf between the ego and the soul is about *finding balance*. We know that we are personalities (egos), yet we know also that we are all unique reflections of Divinity. When we rise above our self-focused, mundane-life-distracted egos and strive to love everyone and everything unconditionally, we can embrace the

Law of Divine Oneness and transcend the illusion of separation between the physical and spiritual worlds. When we consistently reach for higher planes of awareness, and confirm that we are one with the ALL, our ego can be more easily managed and directed towards supporting our spiritual pursuits. And, when our ego is not self-focused, it becomes increasingly heart-centered and unity-minded. So, while the ego is fixated with life in the physical world, we can aspire to 'get the ego on board' with helping us to live a more spiritual, holistic, ONE-focused existence. While the ego would like us to believe that we are separate, special, and superior, in truth we are all—human beings, animals, insects, and so on—equal in the eyes of the Divine creator. In this debate, ego's perspective is erroneous, only the soul's perspective reflects the truth.

The ego can be a dangerous master or it can be our faithful servant. So, ultimately, our goal is not to destroy the ego, it is rather to embrace the ego as a tool to master the spiritual lessons we came to this physical plane to learn. It is about maintaining balance and harmony between mind (ego) and spirit as they both serve our ever-expanding Divine consciousness.

Our ego can also serve us by allowing us to believe in and love ourselves enough to pursue our dreams with confidence. However, if the ego becomes unbalanced and we become willing to hurt or to take advantage of others to reach our goals, then we are not vibrating in harmony with our highest potential nor are we allowing space for the universe to work with us in obtaining our goals. If we allow our egos to hold a "lack" mentality or we allow the ego to convince us that we are "not good enough," we are coming from a place of fear, and when we are in fear, we are not living with full faith, trusting in the universe. This sends a 'signal' into the ethers that the universe cannot deliver what we desire.

In order to ensure that our ego does not get in the way of our Divine alignment, we must first trust that the universe is indeed on our side. We must also endeavor to maintain harmony between our ego and our soul. When our ego and soul are working in harmony, the universe conspires to serve our greatest needs. When we transcend our ego's perception that we are separated from All That Is, and tap into our soul's perception that we are a part of a greater whole, life begins to unfold in miraculous ways. When we do this, we get out of our own way and we master the ego. And, when we are masters of our egos we can choose at any point how we will carry our energy and how we will project it into the world and onto those around us. Thus, rather than allowing our egos to be obstacles preventing us from moving into our best, soul-based life, we can tame the ego, broaden our perspectives and expand ourselves outward to embrace a larger life—the life of universal consciousness.

Ten Ways to Tame Your Ego:

1. Be humble. Realize that you are a small part of the whole, vast universe. Humility will always serve to balance the ego.

2. Be generous. When your ego flares, take time to give to a cause or to people. Whether it is just being present unconditionally and listening, or donating time to support others' needs, honoring others and providing service to others brings everything into perspective.

3. Do not judge. Check in on your judgements of others. If you judge someone, you are projecting that you are better than them. Remember, everyone has something to offer in this human experience, and even if we don't fully understand someone's purpose, we must learn to love and accept others for who they are.

4. Be grateful. Always try to maintain a state of gratitude. Others have helped you to get where you are, and whether their influence was "good" or "bad," they helped you to become who you are today. When you are seeking balance in your life, holding an attitude of gratitude is always the best choice.

5. Be open. Always keep your heart and your mind open to new perspectives. If we are not rigid in our thinking, we can embrace new perspectives and use them to expand our minds and to grow as spiritual beings having a human experience.

6. Think before you speak. Remember: Your words can lift or lower someone, they can hurt or help—so always use your words with love and integrity.

7. Be quietly confident. Someone who is confident does not need to brag, gloat, or put others down. Cockiness, on the other hand, is a sign of weakness and a desire to seek attention and assurance from others.

8. Be compassionate. Where competition once served you, now cultivate compassion. Look at others as friends and fellow travelers, not as strangers or rivals. Ask yourself not "What can others do for me?" but ask instead, "How can I help?"

9. Live from your heart. In everything you do, ask yourself, "What is my intention right now? Is my heart driving me or am I acting from my ego?"

10. Learn to laugh at yourself. Humor is a wonderful way to break up with the out-of-balance ego! Why take life seriously? After all, not one of us is getting out of here alive!

Self-Love and Spiritual Prosperity

> "For eons, humanity has knelt to kings and queens, we have given our divine connection to priests and prophets. Now, we're seeking our own truth and living through the frequency of our hearts. We know that all beings are part of the divine and that love transcends all things."
> —Chantelle Renee

Most people have struggled (or are still struggling) with loving themselves unconditionally and have exceedingly high expectations of themselves. The constant struggle between not-being-good-enough and striving to be better-best-greatest pulls us out of alignment. It makes us doubt that we are truly eternal, unique expressions of *God*/Source; it prevents us from living the life we desire, filled with love and abundance. By embracing our imperfections as gifts for reflection and self–transformation, however, we can empower ourselves to transmute negative, harmful energy into positive, purposeful energy. Like the alchemists of ancient times, we can transform the lead of our faults and failings into the gold of self-empowerment and self-love.

As noted earlier, when we first arrive on the earth plane as babies, we are pure *God*/Source energy in physical form. Then, we begin to absorb the world's views unconsciously, we develop belief systems concerning who we are, and we classify and categorize ourselves based on our race, gender, religion, capabilities, financial status, family of origin, etc. We build our identity around these perceptions and we become products of our environments.

As also noted earlier, as we grew up, we adopted others' thoughts about us as our own, without question. For example, if someone called us stupid or ugly, that term became a part of our self-talk. We drew these hurts into our hearts and minds, we collected them one by one over time, storing them up in our psyches like misers amass coins, allowing these wounds to create and define us, without consciously knowing that the insults others projected towards us were in truth about them and their own pain and self-loathing. When people project negativity or judgements, it is as if they are projecting their own inner shadows outward, often times unconsciously. When people are hurt, they hurt others.

Many who suffer today with feelings of low self-worth or self-hatred have never been shown a real example of what unconditional self-love looks like. For the most part, the members of our families of origin who taught us low self-worth instilled in us what they knew—they did not experience self-love in their childhood, either. So, pointing fingers and blaming your parents for your emotional wounds does not serve anyone. We can only teach what we know.

Children, free spirits that they are, need discipline to encourage them to behave in societally-mandated ways. Many children, however, were disciplined by parents who were less-than-perfect, and the process of discipline became instead punishment and rejection. Many of us felt love being withheld from us for our behaviors and this planted a seed within our subconscious minds that love is conditional: love must be earned. We began to accept that we were not lovable and that in order to be loved, we must conform to others' ideals. So, rather than our parents' discipline having made us into better people, it set the foundation for life-long self-loathing and diminished self-esteem.

All the hurt within our lifetimes has served us in many ways that may be hard for our human minds to understand. It has allowed us to feel the emotional depths of pain, lack, fear, insecurity, self-loathing, depression, loss, sadness, grief, despair, and so on. That is the gift those who have hurt us have given us!

How can we know the heights of love unless we have understood the depth of pain? How can we master unconditional love unless we have experienced the polarities of all versions of love: messy love, crazy love, intoxicating love, painful love, loss of love, lack of love?

Our lives are meant to be felt deeply—the positive, the negative, and everything in between. At birth, we were pure, unconditional, loving energy. Those who have hurt us and wounded us have given us the tools to start our journey back to our true essence as the unconditional, Divine love whence we came. Only through being deeply emotionally wounded can we possibly find our way out of the shadows and back to the light of the Divine. Our wounds and the scars they leave us with are not weaknesses, they are gifts of strength. They test our grace, they bring us a breadth of wisdom that can only be gathered out of the depths of pain.

Does this all make sense to you? Your wounds are your gifts! They are your pre-paid tickets back to Divinity. Every person who said a hurtful word, didn't show up, lied to you, or intentionally offended you has gifted you with the opportunity to get to know yourself and fill yourself with the love that is already yours. You had forgotten—their actions were your reminders. "Ha," you might say, "that may be true for others, but not for me." But....

It is prudent to remember that none of us are perfect, and just because someone hurt you, or did not love you the way you wanted or needed them to, does not mean they did not love you the best they could at that time. Yes, perhaps they were selfish, self-centered, greedy, mean, etc. —but that was the reality they were operating within, that is how their own wounds manifested for them at that time. There was a cosmic dance taking place, and you were both a part of that dance. You may not have danced willingly in your physical awareness, but the soul part of you rejoiced in the dance for it knew that this interaction was pre-destined—it was a soul contract you signed—an opportunity that you yourself had arranged in order for your soul to grow exponentially.

But you have forgotten your soul contracts, and now those human interactions that hurt you are shadows of the past. Time has passed, yet you still find yourself in a negative pattern of seeking the love from others that you did not receive in your growing-up years. Fantastic! Recognizing this is the first step on the journey to self-love. It is equally important to realize that when we project our expectations upon others to love us in the way we want to receive their love, we actually prevent love from flowing freely to us. Instead of healing our emotional issues and clearing blockages, such expectations continue to hold us back.

The real key to being loved the way you want is to seek *self-love*, to tap into your innermost self. Remember that baby-self we talked about earlier? Feel that innocent love generating outward from deep within you. Visit with babies, play with them, feel the unconditional, joyous love that they exude—and then turn inward and find that love within yourself. It is there, it always has been. Tap into it and it will begin to flow—in fact, your heart will overflow—and you will no longer look to others to love and care for you.

We each have everything we need in the depths of our own being. But if we look outside of ourselves for love, we will never find what we are seeking. Seeking fulfillment from an outside source will always leave us empty until we fill the holes within ourselves with unconditional self-love. Seeking love and acceptance from others before you have found it within yourself will always leave you insecure and disempowered.

Once we become unconditionally loving, we release resistance. The foundation for self-mastery is to truly love yourself deeply, so that you can give and receive love freely. It is so freeing to love yourself deeply, to transcend your insecurities and to let go of all that no longer supports you!

"You have been criticizing yourself for years and it hasn't worked. Try approving of yourself and see what happens."
—Louise L. Hay

Take the Other Road

It all sounds great, doesn't it—loving yourself wholly and fully, being confident in the world, and flowing unconditional love out to everyone around you? But after having experienced severe trauma, emotional abuse, physical abuse, sexual abuse, bullying as a child, etc., we are left with wide-open emotional wounds that set the stage for enduring self-hate and ultimate self-destruction. The idea that we could ever rise above this depth of pain and sorrow and tap into our 'own-baby-love' just sounds artificial, not to mention impossible. After all, we have been the victims of others' cruelty, selfishness, unkindness, heartlessness, etc. All of that is true and it is a great excuse to continue down the path of self-hatred—even though you know it can lead only to further despair, sadness, and the certain failure of all your life's hopes and dreams. There is another road you can take, however, and this alternate route leads surely to hope, happiness, and the fulfillment of your dreams. If you are interested in taking this alternative route, it is simple to get from where you are onto that road—all you need to do is make one key decision:

FORGIVE.

Before you dismiss this idea out of hand—perhaps you think that the crime committed against you was too heinous, that the wound imprinted upon you is too deep, that "they" are too cruel, too selfish, that they do not deserve it, etc.—think on this one thing:

Forgiveness is not for the other person.
Forgiveness is for you.

Forgiveness allows you to transcend the pain and anger you hold about your wounds. You cannot change the past, and forgiveness instantly clears the blockages that are stopping you from moving forward. Forgiveness is a primary part of the process of learning how to give unconditional love as well as to receive it. Forgiveness opens your heart so that love can flow freely from you and to you—and when love is flowing to you and from you, magic happens—and dreams come true. So, try it just once—open your heart, and forgive those who have hurt you.

> "What tried to demolish me I allowed to polish me."
> —India Arie

Open Your Heart

> "One open heart has the power to ignite many hearts."
> —Chantelle Renee

Here is an affirmation to assist you in opening your heart. (When you do this exercise, consciously expand your aura, and visualize your heart chakra opening wide.)

> *"I love myself deeply, so that I can love freely. I am filled with love. It pours effortlessly through me, gracefully, into eternity. I am love."*

Here is another affirmation you can use to help you open your heart and get in touch with the self-love within you. I wrote this as I observed several teens entrapped in taking selfies, completely disconnected from their present moment and their surroundings. They were seeking self-love and acceptance from others virtually, instead of connecting with those who were with them in the moment. That scene inspired me to write this:

> *As I look in the great mirror before me, I see a spiritual being that came to experience physicality. I must not get lost in the limited mask of this temporal reality. I love this gift of life that creation has bestowed upon me. I draw not only upon the strength of the physical body that envelopes me, but also upon my spiritual wealth, the eternal spring that brings forth all Divinity.*
> —Chantelle Renee

As I watched the teens interact with the people on the other end of their cell phones via Facebook or Twitter or Instagram or Snapchat—wherever they were—I realized that there was so much that the wise part of me wanted to share with them. I wanted them to know that the photos and messages they felt obligated to send were drawing them outside of the present moment, outside of themselves, into a realm of "otherness." I wanted to tell them that comparing yourself to others will always leave you in despair. I wanted to say, "You will never be them and they will never be you. Envy and jealousy are lower vibrational emotions and our goal is to live as much as we can on the higher vibration of appreciation and admiration. And to live in gratitude and admiration, you have to live in the *now*. There is no need to prove yourself to anyone. There is no need to clamber to the top of the popularity pile! There will always be someone more beautiful, wealthier, famous, popular. Let it go! None of that will go with you at the time of your return home back to Source. At the end of your life you will be most grateful for the love you gave and received, for the memories, and the experiences. No material or physical gain goes with us!"

I wanted to tell those teenagers that when they let go of doubt and insecurities, they can begin to love their layers of shame, self-hate, fear, and judgement so much that they all begin to dissolve in the light of love. I wanted to ask them, "Do you choose to love yourself unconditionally? Or do you choose to remain in your pain?" I wanted them to know that healing comes from being in an open and vulnerable space of complete surrender and transparency, right here, right now. I wanted them to know that to love yourself is to love creation itself, to know your Divinity expressing itself through this temporary human physicality. I wanted to encourage them to embrace their soul's uniqueness, to tell them that each of them are a gift to the ever-expanding consciousness of humanity and the cosmos, a Divine expression of all that is and all that is to come. I wanted to tell them, "Open your heart to the greatness that is you."

There were two more important lessons I wanted to share with them, but the teenagers were, of course, lost in their digital worlds and would not have heard this sage advice from an adult whom, they would certainly have thought, didn't know anything about their lives! So, instead of conveying this wisdom to them, I share it with you, dear reader.

1. *Always be yourself!* Embrace your uniqueness, it is your soul's signature! Being yourself in all your interactions with others can be challenging, especially when our modern society so freely encourages judgement, promotes sameness, and discourages those who are distinct or unique in their looks, occupations, lifestyles, etc. But if you can find the courage within yourself to be authentic in all your dealings, this is a wonderful step towards freeing yourself from your personal prison of pain. We can often feel that it is weak to be open and vulnerable with others—that such openness and transparency leaves us defenseless, feeling naked,

an easy target for scrutiny or judgement. However, the powerful act of being vulnerable creates a space within us for unconditional love to flow freely through us and out into the world and beyond, into the cosmos. Your vulnerability is an invitation for *God*/Source to infuse your insecurities with unlimited potential for growth and expansion. Your vulnerability is sacred, it is fueled by integrity, and leads to self-discovery and mastery.

Being vulnerable frees us from living from our ego-selves. So, *be you* unapologetically, embrace your authenticity. If we can't be vulnerable with ourselves, we can't be vulnerable with others, either. Vulnerability and transparency are the keys to living your life authentically. Being vulnerable brings us face to face with our shadow-selves, it helps us to deal with our unresolved emotions, overcome our insecurities, and open our hearts. Until we can live life authentically, we will remain motivated by the fear-driven ego. When we find the courage to be vulnerable, we commit to feeling our pain, facing it, embracing it, and healing it.

2. *Be aware, always, of the Vanity Trap.* We are all imperfect—as the famous entrepreneur and owner of *The Body Shop*, Anita Roddick, once said, "there are eight women in the world who look like super models and three billion that do not." If you are one of the three billion, remember that getting caught comparing your level of beauty to the eight supermodels is a trap that sets up resistance to embracing and loving who you are right here, right now. Do not become overly focused on the you who is made of material stuff, you may miss out on the spiritual life that is unfolding magically before you and within you.

When we become body-focused, we limit our spiritual experience. We all can find something imperfect in ourselves—if we seek it, we can surely find it. We all look to others and admire attributes that others have that we wish we had. Keep in mind that those whom you are admiring may dislike the very attribute in themselves that you perceive as perfection. Beauty truly is in the eye of the beholder. Take pride in yourself and take care of yourself, but do not cling too tightly to the physical shell that encases your soul. This body you live in is only borrowed temporarily, it does not define who you are, it is a physical vessel that allows your spirit to explore the physical plane. By embracing your perceived imperfections as gifts for reflection and spiritual expansion, you have the power to transform negative, focused energy into positive and purposeful energy, and to transform your rocks into multifaceted gems.

So, stay away from the bathroom mirror—focusing on the appearance of your physical body can be a huge problem. When we focus upon what we perceive as flaws, we amplify them and diminish the gift that our physical bodies are. Remember, our bodies are temporary, our souls are eternal. Society's ideals of beauty are artificial and commercial, they are the product of advertising companies, seeking to increase corporate bottom lines by profiting from your insecurities.

When you do catch a glimpse of yourself in the bathroom mirror, tell yourself, out loud, "You are the love of my life, you are my heaven on earth. You are my best friend, and together we are whole and powerful!"

In so many ways, this human experience can make you feel small, insignificant. But remember, you are not your body, you are an incredible, eternal, perfect expression of the Divine, no less than anyone or anything on this planet. You are here on purpose; you chose this life on the physical plane, right here, right now.

Here is another affirmation to assist you in loving you!

> *I don't strive to be perfect. Where I came from, I already am. I love my imperfections because they make me unique. I am brave and there is freedom in that. I love with all that I am. Vulnerable, I invite others to open their hearts. Life is going to hurt, it's meant to be felt. I am strong and I am powerful. I am thankful for all that I am and all that I have.*

Practice Gratitude

Practicing gratitude has always helped me to find my way back to *now*. The present moment is where we create, where we realize that every outcome in our lives depends upon the actions we take *right now*. Instead of focusing upon lack, focus on the *now*. This will always bring you to focusing on gratitude for what you have in the moment. This is a conscious shift in perception that always results in motivating you to act and create a new outcome!

Here are some reflections on *Gratitude*:

- Gratitude is a super power when you know how to use it.
- Walking your path with your heart filled with gratitude lays the foundation for abundance in all areas of your life; it opens your whole being to the Divine. By remaining in gratitude, you amplify the signal to the universe that you are open to receive more to be grateful for.
- It's important to truly feel gratitude when you focus upon your blessings.
- You always have a choice to be grateful or not. If you feel like you have nothing to be grateful for, start by focusing on gratitude for the sun for providing abundantly for life

to thrive. Be grateful for the moon, the stars, for the earth, and for the grass beneath your feet. Be grateful for your eyes that see, for your lungs that allow you to breathe. Be grateful for your relationships as they offer you companionship. Be grateful simply that you exist at all.
- When you stand in gratitude, you lift yourself up by focusing on what you do have, not what you don't have.

"When you give gratitude, your vibration is lifted."
—Chantelle Renee

Embrace Life – Love Yourself!

Rejoice in your place on this earth, embrace creation in its totality. Love all of your shortcomings and inadequacies as extensions of pure source energy. Embrace life in all its fullness and draw your power from eternity in a stream of love. Transform that loving energy into your own unique ray of Divine possibility. Then, use that force of love to manifest your dreams and to become fully who you are.

Remember, love is the most valuable currency available to humanity. You may possess beauty, riches, or fame—but all of these will leave you empty at the end of this physical experience. Your spiritual self will be with you until the day you leave this physical realm (and beyond), so embrace yourself. As we have said, when you love yourself fully and completely, all things will come to you.

Four Practical Exercises to Learn to Love Yourself

- Love yourself exercise #1: Get quiet. Focus on your breath. Feel a rising sense of gratitude for every part of your body—gratitude for your eyes that see; gratitude for your ears that hear; gratitude for your arms that do, and hold, and embrace; gratitude for your legs which take you everywhere you want to go. Focus on all the things about your body that you are grateful for—and there will be no room in your heart for any judgements or thoughts that you are less than perfect. Remember, your energy flows where your attention goes, so feed the true beauty that you are. Hold a place of gratitude inside yourself for you—you are amazing just as you are, here and now.

- Love yourself exercise #2: Your words have the power to lift or lower, heal or hinder. In this exercise, you are going to create consciously with words of gratitude and self-love. Take some space and time for yourself, and with your pen and journal in hand, create a list of every word you can think of that resonates around the theme of gratitude and love. Use a dictionary or synonym-finder if you like. When you have a solid list of words, write a story around each one—record a memory of when you felt gratitude and love for someone or something. Let this be a conversation between you, your soul, and the universe. Really feel the words resonating in your heart. Words are energy in action and they create an emotional reaction. Do you feel your vibration rising?

- Love yourself exercise #3: Mirror work is wonderful for allowing you to bring forth your soul; you can connect with yourself on a deep level, not just superficially. Get comfortable in your favorite chair. For at least five minutes, hold a mirror up to your face. Look into your eyes, and connect to your soul. Bless yourself and tell yourself, "I love you. You are brave, you are strong, you matter, and you are loved beyond measure." Look at your features—your nose, your lips, your eyes, your ears, and reflect on what you think about each one. Then, see them the way the creator within you sees them—as perfect. Recognize that when you perceive that you are imperfect, you are being invited to let go of judgement and to love yourself unconditionally. As you are drawn into the mirror, and you converse with yourself, let go into self-acceptance. You may find it awkward to do this at first, as your mind and inner self-talk creates resistance and even judgement. Just allow what is to be, embrace the discomfort, and eventually, you will come to a place of acceptance.

- Love yourself exercise #4: If you are having a difficult time and are struggling to feel love for yourself, this *Serenity Prayer* is a beautiful tool. Write it down, put it on your bathroom mirror, on your bedside table, or anywhere you will see it. Recite it several times each day.

Serenity Prayer
God, give me grace to accept with serenity
the things that cannot be changed,
Courage to change the things
which should be changed,
and the Wisdom to distinguish
the one from the other...
Amen.
—Reinhold Niebuhr

As you go about your day, keep this poem in your mind. Stay true to who you are. Don't get lost in others' perceptions or opinions. Continually bless yourself and others. Accept what you cannot change.

Create Your Future

Not everyone will understand your journey in life. That is fine; it is not their journey to make sense of. This is YOUR experience! It is not for others to tell you how to live or how to experience all of the challenges and victories you will encounter along your journey. Remember, you are the creator of your own destiny / reality. Do not give your power to others, do not allow others to decide how your future will unfold. By all means, take wise counsel, and consider whether the experiences of others resonate with you enough to include variations on their ideas in your life's plan. But above all, remember, this is your life! Have fun creating YOUR future.

In walking your path in life, you must accept that many of the people you walked with early on may not finish with you. Become comfortable with walking your path alone, and trust that those who are meant to walk beside you will come into your life at the right time. Remember always, you are loved unconditionally and you are guided by the light of the Divine. It's truly a gift to be here and to create in tandem with the infinite, cosmic energy of the Divine Source. Create freely!

9

Creating with Emotion

> "As we tune into our own thoughts and emotions, we can shift into the direction of our true intentions. It is at this point that we enter the space of creation."
> —Chantelle Renee

Learning to create with your emotions is a potent way to regain power over your life. Becoming aware of and attuned to your emotional state will serve you well as you move forward on your quest to become master of your destiny.

It is said that the heart is the *seat of emotions*. The principal human emotions which abide in the human heart are Love and Fear. All other emotions stem from either love or fear, and it is from these primary emotions that the entire spectrum of emotions emanates. Our emotions each have a unique frequency and when any one emotion is amplified—when we feel something deeply—that emotion vibrates outward, creating a reaction in the quantum field. Much like a stone thrown into a pond, the emotion ripples outward, generating a vibrational field which influences everything in its path.

As noted earlier, the heart has been documented as being the strongest generator of both electrical and magnetic fields in the human body. Whereas we have been taught that the brain is the generator of power in the body, science now knows that while the brain does have both electrical and magnetic fields, the frequencies they emit are relatively weak compared to the heart's.

Fear has a low, slow, contracting frequency, whereas love has a high, rapid, expanding frequency. Thus, fear is a restrictive emotion and love is an expansive emotion.

When we are in a state of fear, we are out of balance, limited, constrained, and separate. When we are in a state of love, on the other hand, when we are focused on finding balance, we are essentially using the vibration of love to feel our way back to Oneness with the Divine. As we expand into love, we step into the universal flow with the least resistance to our greatest potential; we step into our power as creators. As we practice consciously invoking and amplifying higher vibrational emotions, as we guide them in the direction of our intentions, we send powerful signals of gratitude rippling out into the universe. In these modern times of expanding consciousness, those seekers who live with awareness can move at an accelerated rate through these higher frequency energies and thereby can develop their energetic and spiritual strength. When you use the vibration of love to connect with the Divine Source, just as the water rippling out from a stone dropped into a pond eventually returns to the source of impact, so, too, your ripples of gratitude will return to you what you send out. It's the law.

Epigenetics and Your Emotional World

The science that studies how the development, function, and evolution of biological systems are influenced by forces operating outside the DNA sequence—including intracellular, environmental, and energetic influences—is called *epigenetics*. The revolutionary research and insight of Dr. Bruce H. Lipton, twenty-first century stem cell biologist and a pioneer in the study of epigenetics, has revealed that we are not simply victims of our genes. Dr. Lipton, best known for promoting the idea that genes and DNA can be manipulated by a person's beliefs, is leading humanity onto a new path of empowerment. We can, he says, reclaim dominion over our bodies, which in turn will allow us to recover our natural healing abilities and perhaps even turn our new millennium medical paradigm on its head.

According to the science of epigenetics, it's your perception of your environment that controls your genes. Your thoughts and emotions, in other words, have a direct effect on your cellular structure!

For example, scientific research has linked the human capacity for emotion to our DNA. It is now believed that our base emotions directly affect our DNA and, in turn, influences the physical world we create and experience. Without elaborating on the complicated science behind DNA Codes, essentially what this means is that, for example, a human being living in fear is vibrating at a low and slow vibratory frequency and that person exists in a state of stagnation and may be prone to illness. A human being living in the pattern of love, on the other hand, is vibrating at a higher frequency and that increased resonance offers the greatest potential for well-being and healing.

Thus, when we are living in love, we are resonating with higher frequencies, and this is how we raise our consciousness. Those who resonate with the lower emotional states, on the other hand, the so-called "survival emotions"—fear, hate, greed, and envy—remain in stasis, shut down energetically and spiritually.

Now, the idea that our feelings, our emotions, and how we perceive our environments affects us on a cellular level may be a leap for many people. If none of it seems possible to you, sit with that resistance. Ask yourself, "Why do I feel that this could not be possible?" If we can allow ourselves to think without engaging with the preconceived notions placed on us by our families, our cultures, our religions, our societies, our teachers, etc.; if we can transcend these limits and boundaries and instead adopt a "quantum perspective;" perhaps we can embrace the idea that our minds truly can control matter. If this is true, you might ask, does it mean that we have to accept the ailment and disease in our bodies? What if we were born with a limitation such a missing limb or a mental impairment? Does this mind-over-matter theory also mean that we are capable of reversing any disorder of the body or any malformation?

The answer, in a word, is "Yes!"

This may be a little unbelievable, and perhaps not even conceivable for most people. Biologically speaking, however, regeneration is the process of renewal, restoration, and growth that makes genomes, cells, organisms, and ecosystems resilient to natural fluctuations or events that cause disturbance or damage. Every species is capable of regeneration, from microorganisms to mammals. A starfish can grow back a limb, for example, a lizard can grow back its tail, spiders can regenerate their legs, deer can regrow their antlers—just to name a few. There is a lot of untapped intelligence within our DNA and cellular structure, so it seems wise for us to remain open to the possibility that we, as human beings, might be able to align ourselves to a regenerative state of being as well.

However, before we can do this, we must leave our limited beliefs in the past and step into whole new way of thinking. What if this potentiality exists? What if we could all change our mindsets and believe that, personally and collectively, we might be able to bring forth a new way of experiencing being a human being?

Reprogramming our subconscious minds is different than reprogramming our conscious minds. Our conscious minds are creative and are freely connected to Source. They can grasp things more quickly. The subconscious mind, on the other hand, does not work this way. It can, however, be reprogrammed through practice, repetition, and/or hypnosis to form new habits. The subconscious mind is like a computer—it can be programmed. So, to truly make shifts in our fundamental human beliefs, it will take real effort, pure intent, and dedication until we can fully accept that we human beings are powerful in ways we cannot even imagine—all we need to do is program that power into our subconscious minds—and we may become super-human!

Here is a quote I really like from Dr. Bruce Lipton:

> *Because we are not powerless biochemical machines, popping a pill every time we are mentally or physically out of tune is not the answer. Drugs and surgery are powerful tools when they are not overused, but the notion of simple drug fixes is fundamentally flawed. Every time a drug is introduced into the body to correct function A, it inevitably throws off function B, C, or D. It is not gene-directed hormones and neurotransmitters that control our bodies and our minds; our beliefs control our bodies, our minds, and thus our lives ... Oh ye of little belief!*
> —Bruce H. Lipton
> *The Biology of Belief: Unleashing the Power of Consciousness, Matter and Miracles*

The Tyranny of Emotion

Dr. Lipton also points out that "We are not victims of our genes, but masters of our fates, able to create lives overflowing with peace, happiness, and love." This means that not only are we responsible for all the moments of our lives in which we are feeling uplifted and experiencing positive emotions, we are also responsible for all of those moments in which lower-vibrational emotions such as sadness and fear affect our day-to-day realities.

Sadness, fear, and other negative emotions have great power to paralyze us and keep us from living our lives fully. Fear especially can keep us in a restrictive energetic state. It is often said that FEAR is simply false evidence appearing real. We need to gain control over our fear and allow it to serve us instead of rule us. Fear is an illusion that our mind creates to keep us from expanding. If we can master our minds, we can master our lives.

For example, we must live life being practical and cautious—we can't, for example, jump off the top of a building and expect that we won't be injured or killed. So, we listen to our inner guidance and instincts—they are our inner navigational system and we sense those instinctual feelings as fear. But whereas this instinctual fear serves us and is a natural process, unnatural fear does not serve us. We must find clarity by distinguishing natural fear—the fear stimulated when we are in real danger—from false fear (unnatural fear), the fear that holds us back from resonating fully with our true selves and preventing us from finding our true purpose.

We must face false fear head on, and when we do, we will find ourselves living our lives more fully, doing things we never thought we could do. Indeed, life is meant to be felt and experienced—in all its facets—and this means that we must be present with both our good and our bad feelings.

Some psychologists debate whether or not all of the emotions we human beings experience are true *emotions*, per se, arguing that there are only six (some say eight) true emotions—happiness, sadness, fear, anger, surprise, and disgust. In our interpretation, there are numerous emotions and states of consciousness and we include many of them on our Emotional Scale.

The figure below and the emotional scale we present later in this chapter are both adapted from Esther and Jerry Hicks' *Emotional Scale*, from their best-selling book, *Ask and it is Given*.

"I once swam in shallow waters only to get caught up in the rocks and mud. Now, I dive deeper and feel freer."
—Chantelle Renee

The river diagram below represents how human emotions can be in a free-flowing and allowing state as well as in a contracted and stagnant state.

Positive emotions and feelings. High and rapid vibrational frequency, expanding energy. (center of the river)

Negative emotions and feelings. Low and slow vibrational frequency, contracting energy. (sides of river, rocks and mud)

THE FLUX AND FLOW OF HUMAN EMOTION AND FEELINGS

As you can see, there are good-feeling emotions and bad-feeling emotions. When it comes to learning how to manage our emotions, making them work for us instead of against us, it is important to remember that a good-feeling emotion is not *better* than a bad-feeling emotion per se, for all emotions allow us to *feel*. When we feel, we create. To bring forth our feelings is to bring forth transformation and healing.

The rendering above showing free-flowing and contracting emotional attributes can help you feel your way back into the present moment. How are your emotions making you feel, here and now? Are you "stuck" in a feeling you want to change? When you become consciously aware of your thoughts and emotions you can shift them into the direction of your intentions. It is at this point that you empower your creativity.

The Power of Feeling

If we can truly *feel our feelings* without judging ourselves, we can liberate ourselves from the tyranny of being driven to action by our feelings. Instead of our emotions leading the way, we can allow them to guide us and use them in a purposeful, powerful way. The trick is to not remain anchored in any one emotion for too long, and each time an emotion arises, to just be present with it, to allow it to flow through us, to be open and receptive, to feel it, and to let it touch our hearts and observe it. When we let our feelings flow, instead of resisting them, we naturally return to a state of happiness.

So, according to this philosophy, from wherever you are in any moment—you can *feel* your way to happiness. It doesn't matter if you are angry, sad, afraid, or whatever—all you need to do is *pivot*. Pivoting is another concept popularized by Esther and Jerry Hicks. It works like this: when you are engaged in thinking about what you don't want—to do, or to have, or to feel—*pivot*. Just transfer that thought to thinking about what you do want—to do, or to have, or to feel. Pivoting helps you to get into a positive space and put your energy into creating positive thoughts to attain a positive outcome.

Remember, *what you focus on increases*—so focus on the positive. And whenever you catch yourself slipping into negative thought patterns—pivot!

Esther and Jerry Hicks developed a great way to pivot with your feelings too, using what they call *The Emotional Scale*. Whatever you are feeling right now, feel it, and then step up to the emotion that comes above it on the scale below. As they point out in their book, *Ask and It Is Given: Learning to Manifest Your Desires*:

> *Within 17 seconds of focusing on something, a matching vibration becomes activated. And now, as that focus becomes stronger and the vibration becomes clearer, the Law of Attraction will bring to you more thoughts that match. At this point, the vibration will not have much attraction power, but if you maintain your focus longer, the power of the vibration will become further-reaching. And if you manage to stay purely focused upon any thought for as little as 68 seconds, the vibration is powerful enough that its manifestation begins.*

So, for example, say you are feeling *irritated*, item #14 on the list below. In this exercise, your task is to feel that feeling, and then step just one step upward on the scale, to item #13, *apathy*. Ask yourself, "What part of this irritation I feel is really founded in apathy?" Now, feel that irritation and apathy, *really feel it*. Once you have a lock on feeling irritated or apathetic, ask yourself, "What part of this feeling is really based in contentment (#12) or intrigue (#11)?" Now, feel that. You get the gist of it. Keep stepping up the scale of emotions, keep spiraling upward and you'll eventually find yourself grounded right in your center of feeling, where love and happiness abide—in your heart space.

The Emotional Scale

Our individual vibration contracts and expands according to our emotional state. When we are in a low, slow emotional vibration, for example, we may feel depressed, hopeless, angry, hateful and so on. This is because we are broadcasting a low, slow signal into the cosmic sea of energy. The universe responds to that vibration and simply mirrors it back to you. The same is true of high emotional vibrations—your signal of happiness, joy, or love is sent out and returned to you. The higher your vibration is, the faster synchronicities will appear in your life, the quicker manifestations will be for you, and the sooner you can achieve inner peace.

The slower your vibration is, on the other hand, the more likely it is that you will become stuck in that vibration, the more you may spiral downward and build greater resistance around yourself. You can think of it as quicksand. If you get stuck in a pit of quicksand, you can get out much faster if you are at the top of the pit than if you have fallen deep into the pit. By being "unconditionally present" with your emotions, you can create a non-resistant state of "allowing." By doing this, you will always be mindful of your emotional state and will always be able to choose what emotion you want to radiate into the universal field—instead of your emotions choosing you! As you practice being present with your emotions, over time, it will become easier to maintain your emotional well-being. Surrender into your emotions and feel yourself rising above all that holds you back!

As you review the emotional scale below, consider that wherever you are on the scale, it will just take one tiny step to reach the emotional state above where you are. So, just accept where you are on the scale, be mindful, and allow the emotion one step higher to flow into your energy field—and allow the emotion you are in to flow away. Step by step, you'll find yourself flowing upward and arriving at the top of the scale—where you'll feel ecstatic and empowered and draw all positive things into your life.

Free-Flowing Upward

These emotions/feelings are *expanded* emotions. They have high energy and a high frequency:

1. Ecstasy
2. Love
3. Happiness
4. Joy
5. Gratitude
6. Excitement
7. Passion
8. Intention
9. Belief
10. Hope
11. Intrigue
12. Contentment

Fluxing and Contracting Inward

These emotions/feelings are *contracted* emotions. They have low energy and a low frequency:

13. Apathy
14. Irritation
15. Failure
16. Skepticism
17. Blame
18. Anger
19. Hatred
20. Unworthiness
21. Grief / Victimization
22. Fear

As we noted earlier, our hearts are our electromagnetic powerhouses. If we can focus and amplify the positive emotions of gratitude, joy, and abundance that originate in our heart center, we can override all negative emotions and align ourselves with the emotional intelligence of the Divine.

To guide your emotions, you need to observe your feelings with love, gratitude, and non-judgement. Don't fear your dark emotions; bring them into the light. Let them become shining guides on your path. Then, you can begin to live your life from love and to resonate with your higher self.

When we are not in alignment with our higher self, we can live our lives unconsciously, allowing our emotions to control our actions. This can leave us anchored in a heavy emotion rather than moving forward to our best selves. It is important, however, not to push your emotions away for by being present with yourself and all of your emotions, you bring them into conscious awareness. Life can be both painful and joyful, and living life means *feeling life*. To paraphrase a popular saying, you can let go into your emotions, or you can be dragged along with them.

As your dormant, suppressed emotions are brought to light, you can integrate them—and when you do, they will no longer have power over you. So, access your emotional wounds and illuminate them. Be with them fully and be grateful for the scars that were born from them. You are a powerful healer! From your wounds comes wisdom, from your scars comes strength.

Someone once said that life begins when we step out of our comfort zone—*and it is true!* When we embrace our emotions, our confidence grows. We tap into our souls and become our own masters. We shape our own reality, guide our own destiny, and become one with our higher vibrations.

By claiming supremacy over your shadow emotions, you will be like the phoenix, rising from the ashes. You will shine like the sun; your transformation will have begun!

Solitude

> "Solitude is seductive for the soul. A sanctuary of silence creates the space to hear existence."
> —Chantelle Renee

We all navigate many tides and waves of consciousness in every moment, either consciously or unconsciously. By getting still and silencing our minds, we bring balance and harmony to our awareness. *We become observers, observing.*

So many of us get busy with life and don't take the time to connect with nature or with our higher selves. This dis-connection leaves us energetically fragmented in many ways. Taking time to sit in silence will reward you with spiritual wealth in ways you never could have imagined. When we take the time to be still and to meditate, we allow Divine wisdom to flow into our consciousness. We find great peace in this connection to All That Is And Ever Has Been and we gain a deep appreciation for the present moment. When we create time in our daily lives to sit in stillness, over time, we can be amid the outer noise and chaos of life while remaining calm within. We can hear our own guidance instead of being influenced by others' notions.

Meditation teaches us to keep our hearts open in every situation. Connecting with nature and the higher self gives us the strength to withstand the storms of life.

So, during your practice of silence and stillness, keep your heart open. An open heart connects you to the heartbeat of the infinite, the light of the Divine, and the intelligence of the universe. The wisdom flows to you through the cosmic light, inviting you to reclaim your majesty and embrace your current reality.

10

Law of Attraction

> "I am a seed planter, a conscious farmer. I reap what I sow. What I water will grow."
> —Chantelle Renee

What is the Law of Attraction? As we noted in the brief section on the Hermetic Principles, in short, it is a universal law which states that "like attracts like." The Law means, in summary, that the spiritual, mental, and emotional vibration you put out into the universe will always manifest in the physical world in direct proportion and in direct relationship to what you put out. Said simply, if you're feeling happy, you will manifest things that make you happy. If you're feeling sad, your reality will show you more things to be sad about. The Law of Attraction makes no judgements about *what* you bring into your energy field—good or bad—so, look around you. If you have what you want, you're using the Law of Attraction to your own benefit. If you don't, then to get what you want, you'll need to rework your relationship to "The Law."

Many great thinkers of modern times have propounded the age-old concept of the Law of Attraction. As noted earlier, it first came into twentieth century mainstream thought when author and entrepreneur Napoleon Hill wrote about it in his famous book, *Think and Grow Rich*. Later, personal motivation coach Bob Proctor, film producer Rhonda Byrne, and the late self-help guru Dr. Wayne Dyer were all champions of this idea. Now, the notion has become an integral part of the New Thought movement, with various advocates promoting their own versions of what "The Law" really means. Perhaps the best definition of what the Law of Attraction is comes from Esther and the late Jerry Hicks, the purveyors of *Abraham* wisdom:

> *Everything in your life and the lives of those around you is affected by the Law of Attraction. It is the basis of everything that comes into your experience. An awareness of the Law of Attraction and an understanding of how it works is essential to living life on purpose. In fact, it is essential to living the life of joy that you came forth to live.*
>
> *The Law of Attraction says: That which is like unto itself, is drawn. When you say, "Birds of a feather flock together," you are actually talking about the Law of Attraction. You see the Law of Attraction evidenced in your society when you see that the one who speaks most about illness has illness; when you see that the one who speaks most about prosperity has prosperity.*
>
> *As you begin to understand—or better stated, as you begin to remember—this powerful Law of Attraction, the evidence of it that surrounds you will be easily apparent, for you will begin to recognize the exact correlation between what you have been thinking about and what is actually coming into your experience.*

Aligning with the Divine

Nothing merely shows up in your experience. You attract it—all of it. No exceptions.
—Esther Hicks

So, according to this popular understanding of The Law, we can use the Law of Attraction to manifest all of our desires. We must simply set our intentions to manifest the things we want and the light of the universe will bring it into our reality.

To bring what we wish for into manifestation, we must be ever mindful of what we are focused on. Do we think about material wealth and our lack thereof, or do we think of spiritual prosperity? If we allow ourselves to concentrate on lack, our thoughts, emotions, and daily concerns can take complete control of our lives—and not in a good way! So, start observing your thoughts—do you contradict your positive intentions by using the words "can't," "don't," or "won't?" If you catch yourself going against the current of your affirmative thoughts with words or thoughts that have the vibration of doubt or lack, be mindful. You can begin to transfer your intention towards negative outcomes—simply by focusing on them.

As we become consciously aware of having pessimistic thoughts, we need to transform them into optimistic ones, and then shift them into the direction of our intentions, creating what we want instead of what we don't want. This *awareness* changes everything. However, it takes daily practice to reprogram our subconscious minds to focus on higher thoughts of spiritual prosperity and the goodness in our lives rather than on the many challenges that arise by virtue of living in the material world. But, once we achieve and maintain a state of positive thinking, our imagination and concentration generates creative power.

With our newfound awareness, we take responsibility for the thoughts and the actions that create our experience. We *awaken*, and we remember our true nature as eternal expressions of *God*/Source. As we step into our Divine consciousness, we become creators and the source of our own manifestations.

As we have said before, *what we focus on grows* and *what we resist persists*. Your beliefs, what you love and fear, hope for, or hate—anything your attention is focused on and anything you are resisting is being amplified in your reality, right now. Remember, whatever our human senses can perceive, we can create. As we have seen, the physics of creation really do follow the energy of your thought, and bring what you focus on into physical reality. We attract what we want (and what we don't want!) by who we are being on a continual basis—the universe simply responds to our vibrational patterns. So, if we can expand into Divine love, and consistently experience the joy, gratitude, wonder, imagination, and playfulness that this experience brings, we can leave fear, greed, hate, and envy—and the manifestation of them—behind.

Try to live in the fullness of each minute of your day, and maintain a state of gratitude. Feel in every moment as though you have everything you want; do not acknowledge lack. As we have said before—and it bears repeating, again and again—it is important not only to think about your abundance, but also to *feel* the joy of *having* your abundance, right here, right now—that is what welcomes and anchors the manifestation of your desire in the material world.

So, set your intentions to achieve your best possible outcome, and then surrender. Allow your spirit to guide you, and enjoy the ride. Do not try to control "how" your good will come to you—that simply creates energetic resistance and weakens the force of your intention. Remember, the universe is on your side. Cloak your words and deeds and gratitude—and watch as the universe makes your dreams come true!

Reprogramming

When you begin to work with the Law of Attraction, always expect to get what you desire, whether you are seeking love or laughter, abundance or adventure. And, whatever you wish for, dream big! When you came into this lifetime, you heard "No!" from your parents and those around you frequently. "No" has been programmed into you since birth. Now, you can be creative in un-programming that "No" mindset and reprogramming your mind to say "Yes!" to your highest intentions.

It can be challenging at first to change the "No" mindset to "Yes!" I myself had to accept that low self-worth and lack of self-love were the result of the primary programming I received as a child growing up with working class family who lived paycheck to paycheck. I had to accept that I had adopted a "lack" state of mind. As I learned to love myself, I came to understand that the universe is abundant and that I will always be provided for. Through practicing self-love and gratitude daily, I have broken that resistance and have entered that state of allowing that is a precursor to consciously creating. It was a challenging lesson at times but here, on the other side of it, I realize in retrospect that the universe always had my back.

A Big Adventure that my family and I have experienced over the past couple of years is a great example of how the universe supports us, even when it is testing us. One year, in August, prolonged rainfall in the southern parts of Louisiana—where we were then living—resulted in catastrophic flooding. Thousands of homes and businesses were under water—my family and I lost everything. The water took all of our material possessions; our home needed to be gutted to the studs. We rebuilt from nothing. But that dilemma and its attendant difficulties made us strong, it united us. We had to "Let Go and Let God." We came together as a family, as a community, as a region, and we all had to trust that everything would come to us in Divine timing. We all learned at that time that it is as important to give as it is to receive—and as we embraced our neighbors and members of our communities, and as they in turn embraced us, we all gave freely to one another whatever and whenever we could. This loving generosity created free-flowing abundance for everyone. We all felt such gratitude for everything we had each day, and we all gave freely without fear of losing anything—for we had nothing to lose. From day to day, even though it was sometimes an immense challenge to stay in an abundant state of being, even though we were exhausted and overwhelmed, we practiced gratitude and focused on what we still had—each other. Practicing kindness and patience through all of the frustration and devastation served us well. It is beyond amazing how everything flowed back into our lives.

Life always sends us the most remarkable lessons on our journey towards oneness, lessons that ultimately help to align us with our flow. When we are in a state of flow, trusting that the universe provides and that everything will come to us, we create a clear channel of communication of trust with the Divine. This is hard for our human minds, for our early programming set us up to desire instinctively to know, in detail, how everything will work out. As we said earlier, we have been conditioned to believe that abundance is not our birthright and that lack is our reality. But, when we remain open, when we trust that the universe really *is* on our side, we settle into alignment with our good, and we become magnets that draw our good to us. But remember, you cannot just put your trust out there now-and-then, and sit back and wait. You must set a daily practice of awareness, being mindful that you are always consciously creating your own reality. You must remain grounded in gratitude for all that you already have; you must be thankful for being a part of the magical universe that has allowed you simply to exist at all!

Our wish truly is the universe's command. Whatever we intend to create, we can create. When we master being in a state of knowing (that the universe has our backs!), trusting that knowing, maintaining a state of gratitude, and following it all up with action when opportunities come our way, we bring forth the manifestation of our intentions.

Remember, abundance is our birthright. It is our conditioning as children that makes us feel not deserving of all that we desire. We are Divinity expressing itself, we are far greater than the limitations that others have placed upon us. We know now that what we focus on grows—and if we're focused on celebrity gossip, political propaganda, and all that is perceived to be wrong in the world, things will be chaotic and wrong in our personal lives too. But if we create a daily practice of gratitude, if we send out love to all of the world without judging or participating in the drama, we set up a new vibration, we step into our roles as powerful creators. We bring goodness not only into our own lives, but we send out love and goodness to everyone around us. This is a wonderful foundation for us to build abundance—ours and others'—upon. We transcend our past limitations—and the limitations of the world around us—and we allow the universe to guide us to the heights of creativity.

The time is now for us to reclaim our sovereignty and to begin co-creating with others, *to become—as Mahatma Gandhi and others have said—the change we want to see in the world*. Remember, everything is frequency/energy, so direct your thoughts and actions in the direction of your intentions. Dream Big—imagination is the power behind creation. And, once you have raised your vibration and have tapped into your creative space, trust the universe and seize every opportunity it sends to you—take action and take steps towards the manifestation of your desires. As noted earlier, this takes constant practice and mindful awareness; but this—and only this—is the sure path to mastery, and to consciously creating your own reality.

Above all, remember to play and to have fun! Open your heart and free your mind—all unfolds in Divine time. That is the Law of Attraction.

11

Your Action Plan - Manifesting your Dreams

> "Whatever you want can come to you, wherever you are. Location means nothing, vibration goes everywhere."
> —Abraham (Esther Hicks)

In this chapter, we provide some tips to help you work with the Law of Attraction to manifest your dreams. If you follow the Law faithfully, and put it into practice every day, you will soon see the things you desire flowing to you freely. Remember, whether you are seeking material, spiritual, or physical abundance, your "best currency" will always be your unwavering faith, belief, and trust in the Universe.

Check in with this list every day. Take time to get quiet and meditate on these ideas. Copy your favorite concepts into your journal and carry it with you—and make notes on your deeper thoughts and intuitive reflections as often as you can. Are you ready?

- Remember, you are a spiritual being who came to this physical realm to create the most miraculous of dreams. You are powerful, you are pure Source energy in physical form. You have roots in the physical world, and you have wings to carry you into the spiritual realms. So, embrace your Divine energy now, and direct your energy towards your highest intention. To acknowledge and bring yourself into resonance with the light of *God*/creation within you, use this invocation—the Science of the Spoken word. Affirm that you are one with the unified field of energy. Say:

I AM Universal, I AM eternal, I AM loved, I AM thankful, I AM provided for, I AM worthy, I AM here to create."

- What are your desires, your wishes, your passions? What experiences do you want to have? Take time to reflect deeply. Do not think about what you do not have—remember, the grass is not always greener on the other side of the fence—so think about what *you* truly want. What would fill up your soul?

- Examine your limiting beliefs. Ask yourself, "What are my beliefs? What collective beliefs do I embrace—those of my country, my society, my community, my loved ones? What beliefs have I borrowed from others?" Make an intention to break the chains that bind you—banish the limiting beliefs that shackle you, impede your creativity, and weaken your connection with Source. You must detach from your limiting beliefs in order to experience something new.

- Emotions and feelings play a key part in the way your energy is moving outward, into the unified energetic field. "Connect the dots" in your current reality. Ask yourself, "What emotional states and/or beliefs do I hold that I can see manifested in my current relationship? What emotional states or beliefs have manifested in my current living situation? What emotional states or beliefs have manifested in my current financial situation?"

- Write a clear, detailed list of the things in your life that you are grateful for. Laminate this list, and place it in your shower, on your bathroom mirror, on your bedside table, in your car, on your desk—wherever you will see it on a regular basis. Tune into the frequency of *gratitude*. Feel it. Allow gratitude to radiate from you. Read your Gratitude List, meditate on it, and envision it two to three times each day. Anchor everything you do with gratitude. Gratitude really is a super power—when we know how to use it, life unfolds in miraculous ways.

- Look for the signs the universe offers you. Watch for the doors that open for you in your life—and when you see them, take action, walk through them! Don't deny anything as being "just coincidence"—remember, you are working in tandem with the Divine energy field now. The more you accept the signs spirit sends you, the more you embrace them, the more the energy quickens, the more good unfolds in your life, and the more manifestations are revealed.

- Make conscious efforts to *raise your vibration*. As we flow with the universe and pull spiritual energy from higher dimensions, we create at a quicker rate. Remember, time and space are illusions! Everything that ever has been or ever will be is *here and now*, and everything is in a constant state of becoming.

Here are ten ways to effectively and practically expand and raise your vibration:

1. Do a digital detox: take a break from technology.
2. Eat clean, fresh fruits and vegetables and drink fresh water (you can bless it too!).
3. Move your body. Take a walk in nature, barefoot. Stretch and do gentle exercise.
4. Give to others. Give a smile or a hug, and offer your time to others.
5. Meditate.
6. Listen to music. Choose conscious and high-vibe tunes that lift and inspire you.
7. Purge your space—clean and organize your home.
8. Spend time with positive and joyful people, seek communities that are empowering to you.
9. Practice gratitude.
10. Turn off the news!

Here is an affirmation you can use to *Raise your Vibration*. It is designed to take approximately two minutes. Read through it and bring yourself into the present moment!

> *The universe is on my side. *God* lives within me and outside of me, extending love to me effortlessly. I am attracting abundance in all areas of my life. I am creating my experiences with every intention I set. My thoughts flow in the direction of my intentions naturally. I love my imperfections; they offer me reflections. I embrace everyone and everything with an open heart and mind. I am fearless and can handle anything gracefully. I give without expectation. I see the beauty in everything. I find joy in the mundane. I walk with gratitude for my health and vitality. I am strong, I am brave, and I am safe. I love myself deeply, so I can love freely. I am thankful for Mother Earth;*

she provides abundantly. I am free to be authentically me, without apology. I love my family, they teach me responsibility and accountability. My emotions are a Divine gift, here to guide me. I am present, I am eternal, and I am love. I call upon my angels and guides to walk by my side. I am here to thrive.

- Keep doubt in check—your ego and your mind will try to rationalize everything. Observe your thoughts regularly, and, throughout each day, reflect on your predominant mental state. Ask yourself, "How am I expressing my energy?" "What am I focused on?" "How am I feeling?" "Do I feel my abundance fully?" "Or do I feel lack?" As we have noted, the universe responds to our vibrational state and it takes conscious effort to keep our emotional, mental, and vibrational states in check. Have fun, play your role in life—but keep yourself where you want to be—at a high level of vibration, confident, loving, grateful, and happy.

- Think, speak, and act as if you already have what you want. Stay always in a state of becoming. Take "inspired action" to make what you want a physical reality. Start putting real effort towards your intentions!

- Keep your innermost desires and the details of your dreams to yourself. When we share our innermost thoughts, they can become distorted or diluted by others' counter-thoughts or judgements.

- Remember, we are not here to create others' realities or to save others. Everyone is on their own sacred path, and everyone has their own, unique-to-them spiritual lessons.

You will inspire others simply by being the best version of yourself and by allowing your loving energy to flow freely.

- Open your heart, free your mind, and remember: Everything arrives in Divine timing. Maintain a state of flow, do not resist or judge. When we allow ourselves to not need to know how everything will turn out, we create a clear channel of trusting communication with the Divine. As we have said, this is hard for the ego to do, as we possess an innate desire to *know* the how, what, and why of *everything*. Additionally, we have been conditioned to believe that abundance is not our birthright and that, instead, lack is our reality. So, *detach* from *how*, *disconnect* from *outcomes*. Just trust that your good is with you now, and *allow* it to manifest.

- Give freely! Give your time, your money, your love, your smiles, and your hugs. Give what you can, wherever and whenever you can.

During focused manifesting, practice being present, in the here and now. Do not get lost in the future, expecting to receive or achieve something in a forthcoming time. The universe unfolds as we learn to perceive ourselves as *not* trapped in time and space, we draw everything to ourselves *here* and *now*. By thinking of the "future" you consign the "now" to being a component of time and space—and this in turn diminishes the energy of your intention.

Finally, create clear, concise, and intentional manifestation worksheets for yourself. Writing your intentions down anchors them and raises their vibration. So, for example, you might write:

1. I will travel with my family on an epic adventure to India this year.

2. I have financial freedom. I am so thankful that I can live my life's passion and that I am rewarded by peace and prosperity in all areas of my life.
    a. I receive compensation for my talents and efforts.
    b. I travel and share my gifts with others.
    c. I learn new ways of expressing and receiving love every day.
3. I am grateful for the unexpected miracles that are always flowing my way.

12

Conclusion

One of the key messages in this book has been the importance of self-love. It is the fountain from which all self-development and evolution springs. If you do not love yourself first, life's lessons cannot be learned. When you realize that you are made in the likeness of a loving *God*, you can open your heart to all that is Divine and step into your role as an agent of Divine will.

By trusting and listening to your internal, Divine guidance system and by nurturing a channel with the Divine, you become confident, you fall away from fear and walk in faith, knowing that the universe is always on your side.

By cultivating compassion and forgiveness, you become a fount of free-flowing, loving energy—and a magnet for that same loving energy. Practicing forgiveness and non-judgement not only serves you but it also serves the All. Remember—you are a part of one, Divine family—we all are here on purpose. We are all-powerful, energetic beings. Are you ready to step into your Divine energy and live the life of your dreams?

You can do and be and have everything you want in this life! By integrating the empowering principles outlined in this book into our daily lives, and by embracing the insights revealed in this book, we can all manifest abundance, health, and prosperity and navigate our earthly experiences with ease.

But remember—we alone are responsible for our thoughts and actions. Through them, we manifest all the gifts and richness in our lives. Our actions create reactions—we are always in constant communion with the universe. By putting the valuable spiritual awareness gleaned from this book into practice, we can all become conscious creators, *creating*. We can tap into the cosmic energy of the universe and use it to raise our vibrations, realize health and happiness, and manifest our every desire.

This book has given you a basic understanding of how the human body's energetic field communicates and interacts with the Divine, and has explained how your energy field is—essentially—both your heaven and your hell. By nurturing a relationship with your subtle body, you can become even more in-tune with and aligned with the Divine. Through practicing energy awareness, you can be fully accountable for the energy you are giving and receiving.

This book has helped you to realize that your emotional state has the power to lift you or lower you, empower you or enslave you. By learning to be unconditionally present with the flux and flow of your emotions and feelings, you can direct your intentions while accepting your triumphs and tribulations not as aids or obstacles on your path, but instead as precious, loving gifts of the human experience. You can remain grateful for all of your life lessons, knowing that everything is *energy*, everything ebbs and flows, everything is constantly transforming. Going with the flow of the river of life allows you to see and feel things from a place of grace. As you float along on the river of life, instead of grasping for rocks that only hold you back, let go—experience the journey!

When we realize just how precious every one of our life experiences are, and how all the experiences and relationships in our lives are mirrors for our spiritual progression, we break the chains of self-limiting beliefs and free ourselves from the cycle of karmic lessons. As we seek to view everyone and everything as our teachers, we mature spiritually, and become freer to experience life in an open and loving manner.

We have discovered in this book that love truly does transcend all things. We can now seek our own truth and live through the highest, nurturing frequency of our hearts and minds. We know now just how powerful our thoughts and intentions are. And, when we learn to apply our intentions to our everyday reality, we awaken from the illusion that we are separate from the whole of creation. As we learn to create in harmony with universal, Divine energy, we realize that each of us are connected intimately to *All That Is*. Together, hearts united, we can co-create a new and better world. We are creating our own future—and we know now that we are the ones we have been waiting for!

We are our own salvation! Let us ignite each other's lights instead of diminishing them. Let us watch the waves of fire within our hearts blaze a trail to a completely new way of being in this world. Let us create a world in which judgement, envy, fear, and hate are dissolved and replaced with love.

By connecting with others in the highest vibration of unconditional love, we build bridges with one another instead of walls. When we are transparent and authentic with ourselves and one another, we create the space for others to become authentic as well—and we become free from the enslavements of the ego.

We are here to learn to communicate from our hearts and to speak our truths effectively. We are here to transform ourselves and our societies, a process of energetic purging and healing our self-limiting programming. We are here to transcend and anchor a higher energetic frequency, setting down the foundations from which we can birth peace and bring abundance to all.

Together, we are transforming ourselves, one soul at a time—from the inside out. We are no longer detached from our lives, we are no longer on the outside, looking in. We are stepping into our Divine power now, focusing on serving spirit and ushering in a new age in which we live in tandem with our own Divinity. We are the new revolutionaries. *Join the revolution*!

In closing, dear reader, it is my sincere hope that this book will serve you on your spiritual journey. May the wisdom in these pages help you to align with the Divine, even through your darkest days. I hope this book will help you to make your inner world richer and your outer world more abundant. I hope that it will provide you with tools to help you take responsibility for the energy you give out—as well as the energy you receive.

Remember—you alone are the savior you have been waiting for! Using love as your beacon of light, may you always find your way home.

> "That which you have will save you if you bring it forth from yourselves. That which you do not have within you [will] kill you if you do not have it within you."
> —Gospel of Thomas

From my heart,
Chantelle

Works Cited - Reading List

Bruyere, Rosalyn L. *Wheels of Light*. New York: Fireside, 1994. Print.

Dyer, Wayne W. *Excuses Begone! How to Change Lifelong, Self-Defeating Thinking Habits*. Carlsbad: Hay House, 2009. Print.

Emoto, Masuro. *The Hidden Messages in Water*. New York: Atria Books, 2011. Print.

Farrell, Joseph. *Manifesting Michelangelo*. New York: Atria Books, 2011. Print.

Hay, Louise L. *I Can Do It Affirmations - How to Use Affirmations to Change Your Life*. Carlsbad: Hay House, 2004. Print.

Hicks, Esther and Jerry Hicks. *The Law of Attraction - The Basics of the Teachings of Abraham*. Carlsbad: Hay House, 2007. Print.

—. *Ask and it is Given - Learning to Manifest Your Desires*. Carlsbad: Hay House, 2004. Print.

Jenny, Hans. *Cymatics - A Study of Wave Phenomena*. Newmarket: Macromedia, 2001. Print.

Judith, Anodea. *Wheels of Life*. Woodbury: Llewellyn, 2016. Print.

Lipton, Bruce. *The Biology of Belief*. Carlsbad: Hay House, 2016. Print.

Prophet, Mark L., and Elizabeth Clare Prophet. *The Science of the Spoken Word*. Gardiner: Summit University Press, 2004. Print.

Robinson, James M., ed. "The Gospel of Thomas." *The Nag Hammadi Library*. Revised Ed. San Francisco: HarperSanFrancisco, 1990. Print.

The Holy Bible - New International Version. Biblica Inc., 2011. Print.

Wilde, Stuart. *Sixth Sense*. Carlsbad: Hay House, 2000. Print.

Virtue, Doreen. *Angel Therapy*. Carlsbad: Hay House, 2012. Print.

Appreciation

Inspirations and Appreciation:

Thanks to India Arie for her inspiration, always.
   https://www.soulbird.com/

Thanks to Gregg Braden for his inspiration for the *Creating with Emotion* section: https://www.youtube.com/watch?v=X1SMqQH7FJU

Thanks to Gabriel Cousens, for the inspiration for the human energy assimilation diagram: (*Spiritual Nutrition: Six Foundations for Spiritual Life and the Awakening of Kundalini*) https://asksablog.wordpress.com/2013/04/04/full-spectrum-of-energy-assimilation/

Thanks to Nassim Haramein for the inspiration on the *Torus* content: www.theresonanceproject.org

Thanks to the anonymous authors of *The Kybalion* for their wisdom and inspiration: http://www.kybalion.org/

Thanks to Barbara Marciniak for her inspiration, always:
   https://www.goodreads.com/author/show/64205.Barbara_Marciniak

Thanks to Reinhold Niebuhr for his "The Serenity Prayer":
   https://en.wikipedia.org/wiki/Serenity_Prayer

Thanks to the folks who uploaded the useful source material on the *Universal Laws*: http://lawsoftheuniverse.weebly.com/12-immutable-universal-laws.html

Thanks to the folks at Wikipedia for their always helpful source material: https://en.wikipedia.org/wiki/Main_Page

Online Sources

http://htrismegistus.blogspot.ca/2012/02/seven-mighty-principles.html
http://www.puramaryam.de/lawhermes.html

Wise Philosophical Quotes:

- For quotes from Albert Einstein, Mahatma Gandhi, Reinhold Niebuhr ("Serenity Prayer"), Nikola Tesla, Wayne Dyer, Louise L. Hay, Max Planck, Anita Roddick, Stuart Wilde, and the Dalai Lama, please google "*Author Name* Quotations"

Graphic Artists:

Gary V. Tenuta
www.bookcoversandvideos.webs.com

Andrew Kukla
www.artrama.net

Silviya Yordanova
DARK IMAGINARIUM Art & Design
www.darkimaginarium.com

Jonathan Brice Lyman
Art by Jonathan Brice Lyman
www.JonathanBriceLyman.com

Notes

Use this section to record your thoughts, feelings, inspirations, and insights. Happy journaling!

Notes

Notes

Notes

Notes

About the Author

Chantelle Renee is an intuitive writer who helps facilitate transformational healing and spiritual empowerment in others through merging spirituality and science. She has run several home-based businesses that have allowed her to be a dedicated, stay-at-home mother of two children. She has been married to the love of her life since 2000. Chantelle has lived in many U.S. states, and the role of wanderer has given her the opportunity to learn, grow, and expand within many communities—knowing always that our real home is in our hearts. Chantelle's trials and triumphs have inspired her own spiritual growth and she has found her calling and passion in serving humanity by bringing forth the spiritually empowering wisdom in this book.

Author Contact:
Chantelle Renee
PO Box 9052
1760 Wabash Ave.
Springfield IL 62704-9997
www.ChantelleRenee.org

Printed in Great Britain
by Amazon

78548229R00123